A Place Called Alice

Table of Contents

Preface

The idea of compiling some of my work into a published volume never really occurred to me until quite recently. To be perfectly honest I didn't think anyone would care or be the least bit interested in the musings of an over the hill, erstwhile denizen of the North Dakota Prairies. Having said that, and having tested the water so to speak, with a number of friends and acquaintances, and trusting that said friends and acquaintances weren't just mollifying the old man, I decided to give it a go.

My writing, I still hesitate to call it my "work" as it has been for the most part a labor of love, has been described as "nostalgic narrative" which means it's stories of my fond memories. Fond stories of the memories of a man who confesses to being quite idealistic about his past. Perhaps in a future volume I'll include some of the not so fond memories that every existence is heir to. But for now what's already here must suffice. I might also mention that the discerning reader will notice a lack of adherence to a single "voice" and I freely admit the fact. While remembering and writing about my "used to be" I often found myself reliving moments frozen in time from the perspective of my sixty years ago self and consequently the language takes on a different timbre.

I also confess to looking at my "used to be" through glasses distinctly rose in color. If I were to be totally honest with you (and myself) the act of walking to Midnight Mass when it was thirty-five below zero was daunting. And of course I recall the maddening itch of barley beards on my skin, or the way the prairie wind made it so darned hard to pedal my bike. But for the purposes of this endeavor I'll remember the ice crystals in the air outlining the streetlights on the way to Midnight Mass looking like Halos of Angels on Christmas Eve. I'll remember that when those barley beards were so irritating I was with my Grandpa on the farm. I'll choose to recall how very much fun it was to pedal my bike with the wind at my back.

You see my friends, it's all a matter of perspective, and this volume is mine.

I've been of the opinion that most all of my writing is pretty self explanatory if the reader just stops for a moment and puts into context the times and places. But someone pointed out to me that there are people who might not know what a binder canvas is, or who have never seen a threshing rig or a prairie steamer or a railroad cut through the prairie roll. So here's the deal, if I sense that some of you, dear readers, are unable to fathom for the life of you, what is being written about, for you unfortunates I will include a short note of explanation. And if that doesn't suffice? Well, as long as I'm still on this side of the prairie sod you can always give me a call or if you're of a mind you can text or e-mail me. I truly hope you enjoy the effort.

Dennis "Mac" McMahon

Prologue

As one of the very first "baby boomers"I grew up in the North Dakotah of the nineteen fifties. I lived in Alice, a little prairie town, that, like a lot of prairie towns, is mostly gone anymore. It was a time before God got put into the Pledge of Allegiance, a time when portraits of Washington and Lincoln, and a copy of the Ten Commandments in gothic script had an honored presence on the walls at school. World War II was still a part of the short term memory then. It's a family legend that my Great Aunt Clara was supposed to have said "Dat Hitler could'a come to Minneapolis, but by God he's damn lucky he doesn't try to come into Nort Dikotah"

Kids today would more than likely say our lives were boring. Our bicycles only had one speed, baseball bats were made of wood, and you had to check and see that no one else was on the line when you used the telephone that stuck up off the desk like in a nineteen-thirty's movie. It was a time when finding that perfect slingshot crotch in the Box Elder trees behind the Alice Hall was something worth remembering

If someone would have used the words "play date " back then, they would have been looked at like they had two heads. We had to use imagination then, my horse, the one that was killed along with me in the charge up San Juan Hill with Teddy Roosevelt and his Rough Riders, was a lath I pulled from a snow fence down by the lumber yard. Yeah, we had a lumber yard too back then. We were cowboys and adventurers and Visigoths and Vikings, and scientists and explorers riding and running for miles into the country and back again, experiencing our world of farms and ranches, inhabited and abandoned and gravel pits and sloughs and creek beds and ravines and waving grass and wheat fields and the occasional grove of trees under a sky so wide it defied explanation.

We didn't know from wind chill charts back then. If it was cold… well "you better bundle up, 'cause it's a little breezy don'chya know. " It was a time when walking backwards a half a mile to school to keep your face from freezing solid warranted not a second thought. Being from the prairies, the wind was simply a fact of life. It never occurred to me that there might be places where it didn't blow. I remember a time when I was ten or eleven and I saw a picture of a winter scene in New England, where the snow had piled up over a foot on the top of a split-rail fence. My first thought was that it was trick photography, snow just doesn't fall like that.

Goose down and Gore-tex and four wheel drive were concepts we hadn't even imagined. A woolen cap with flaps over the ears and a heavy coat with a collar out of imitation fur and brogans underneath our four buckle overshoes was high winter fashion in nineteen fifty-five North Dakotah.

I guess I never realized how unsophisticated we were, we were like some nineteen forties movie or a Norman Rockwell painting and to tell the honest truth

I miss it.

I miss the honesty, the innocence, the wide eyed naiveté. We've got iPhones and iPads, digital cameras and computers. But we've lost our sense of joy I think, our sense of wonder at it all. To tell the honest truth

I miss it.

You see, for me, from my memory to my heart is…

A Journey of No Distance

Though I am alone and far from there
I have them with me still those things I love.

The winter nights

The Northern Lights

summer's yellow green

the amber gold of fall

and quiet

quiet so quiet almost I feel
I am an interloper in a foreign land

When the crystal shard of a Meadowlark at song
serves it seems
only to define the silence

When the haunting call of an austral bound Canada Goose
vibrates the very ashes of my bones.

And wind.

Wind that prowls a winter night.
Wind for whom power lines
like harp strings tightly strung
resonate in sympathy.
Wind that whispers through thigh high grass
in a reflection of itself.

Though I am alone and far from there
I have them with me still those things I love
because you see
it is a journey of no distance
from my memory to my heart

The Town

Through a Plate Glass Window

I had an uncle on my Momma's side

Actually he was my Gramma's Uncle Joe

Uncle Joe came to Alice

before the town was even there

Around eighteen ninety-eight or so

He'd heard the old N.P.

was gonna build a line through here

In the days of steam the railroad guys

would plat the right-of-way.

They wanted towns spaced just right

so they could take on coal and water

The story goes that Uncle Joe had learned

the line was gonna go through

just a little ways north

of what one day we would know as Alice Slough.

Uncle Joe had always wanted to own a general store.

and he'd been thinking about a place to build it.

So he took a chance

Alice is on what they used to call the "Ladies Line" of the Northern Pacific Railroad. the "Old NP" Because of the names of the towns of Alice, Katherine, and Marion. The train would come through around 9 AM and then around 3:30 PM from the opposite direction. When I was small we had train service five days a week, then it went to three, then two, until finally none.

built it there by the wagon road

just a little ways north of Alice Slough.

And even though the railroad

had platted the town three miles west,

my hometown Alice, North Dakota

sprang up instead by Uncle Joe's store.

Gramma's Uncle Joe ran the "Alice Mercantile"

till the end of World War One.

Grandpa's brothers Ernie and Frank

changed it then in nineteen-twenty to "Kapaun Brother's "

which it remained till the end of World War Two

when in nineteen hundred and forty seven

my Mom and Dad bought the place

Changed the name once more to the Alice Fairway Store.

For over twenty years

that store that I grew up in

was the family business

till my Daddy died in nineteen sixty nine

and though she closed it late that year

my Momma lived in her apartment

in back of the Alice Fairway Store

for more than fifty years.

I was thinking about that store.

The store that I grew up in

and I thought about the coal fired furnace

down in the basement there

with it's stoker door that seemed so doggone big

it could'a been the boiler on a battleship.

Four times a day, sometimes five

my Daddy stoked that furnace in wintertime.

Every shovel scooped and thrown by hand.

PV coal briquettes were what we used.

I always thought that we were really swell

using fancy coal briquettes

not the ugly lignite other people burned.

There used to be a sign on a warehouse wall

down by the NP tracks

a lady in a formal dress

a coal briquette in her white gloved hand.

'Heat your home the modern way' she smiles

heat with PV Coal Briquettes'

I was proud that we were modern too

that we used PV coal briquettes.

They delivered that coal

down a chute with a rusted metal door

those rusty hinges squeaked and squealed

and when the door clanged down

it sounded like the closing hatch

on a diving submarine.

The latch was broke and the door held shut with a piece of baling wire.

Sometimes though the wire broke off

and if the wind was right

that door would flop and clang something fierce

through the winter night.

There was a steel grate in the floor of our store

maybe ten foot on a side

where the heat would rise up from the furnace.

It didn't have no fans or blowers

the air just moving naturally with the temperature

I'd often sit at night in wintertime

look at comic books

tucked up against that furnace grate

my butt end almost blistered

my toes so cold I could barely feel 'em.

The air above the furnace grate would shimmer in the heat

and ten or twelve feet away you could almost see your breath.

The only sound the prairie wind careening through the winter night

and the quiet tick, tick, tick

of the cooling furnace grate.

There were three big lights in our store

hanging down on cords six foot long

one up front

another near the back

and one hung down over the furnace grate.

The globes were glass of creamy yellow white

and you switched them on and off

by pulling on a string with a pasteboard cutout sign hanging from the

end.

Holsum Bread, Fairmont Milk ,and Camel Cigarettes

slowly twisting in the yellow light.

On winter nights

when the store was closed

the light above the furnace grate

was the single one kept the dark at bay.

The world without was deep in shadow

and I was in the centre

in that buttery light

my butt against the furnace grate.

There was something almost intimate to those moments

brought a clarity to things.

I sometimes feel the world has lost it's way

that we're kinda like those pasteboard signs

slowly twisting in the air

above the furnace grate.

The floor inside our store is inch thick maple colored nearly black

with sixty years of oil from the sweeping mix.

It settled over time, our store,

so that when you walk the floor

it creaks and groans

like an old man grousing of his rheumatism.

The entrance door is oak varnished almost black

and in the center there's a beveled glass three foot oval window

a picture of a RedWing boot decaled at the bottom.

There's a closer on that door so it doesn't slam when someone lets it go

and at the top a bell that rings when a person leaves or enters.

When I close my eyes I can hear that door in my mind

sound a signature of those years.

The clicking of the latch

the swishing of the door

the ringing of the bell

and the liquid sssklunk as the door swings shut once more.

Often we could tell who came in

from just the sound of the door

and the creaking of the floor when they walked.

When I close my eyes

a hundred scenes course through my mind.

And a lot of them aren't really scenes at all

until a scent or sound tweaks a memory to truly tantalize.

I used to wonder

why the smell of Red Oil Polish

engendered such a sense of warmth and safety.

Then I recalled

the oaken cabinets in our store

waxed and shining

glowing in the sun streaming through the windows of an afternoon

Or I find myself half smiling

at an open jar of German dills

vinegar curling 'round my nose

like the ones we sold from barrels long ago.

And when the smell of coffee percolates those memories

out of hibernation in my brain

I see the mill that sat at counters end

and ground those beans of Radiant Roast

filled the air with that red brown smell of coffee freshly ground.

I remember too my Daddy

in the apron that I'm pretty sure he wore to bed.

Those crinkles at the corners of his eyes.

With his thinning hair parted down the centre

he looked still like his graduation picture

Pipestone High School

Class of nineteen hundred thirty-seven.

It's the little things.

The things not seen at first

that bring my Daddy into view.

His step so fast I had to run to match it.

The tinkle of the spoon in his coffee cup.

And I see him clear

like he was standing with me now

not just a fragment of a past remembered

when I catch the scent of a burning cigarette

Closed half a century past

our store still stands today

and though the paint is peeling

the plate glass windows still are there

Since I was small I've had the feeling

there was magic in our store

and I think it's mostly true

cause' when I look

through that window glass

I can see my Daddy walking toward the door

and if I shield my eyes

I see Frank and Uncle Ernie

and Grammas' Uncle Joe

in there too.

Halcyon Days

I go back to Alice North Dakota

to our little prairie town

three miles east of the knee deep Maple

two miles north of Alice Slough.

I go back in my heart

to a time before time was blurred

through the prism of ten thousand sundowns.

Cottonwoods stood the sentry then

watched over our prairie town.

Those were the Halcyon Days

streets filled

people passing, talking, laughing.

Behind the false front shoppers crowded

floorboards creaked

The signs said

"Fairway Foods"

and "Fairmont Milk"

and "Radiant Roast Coffee"

And "Did you forget shoelaces?"

above the handle on the exit door

Potatoes and peanuts were in burlap bags

cheese was sliced from a twenty pound round cut with a long blade knife

eggs were in the cooler in a wire basket.

and in the early morning

the fresh brewed coffee smell percolated the very air

and the only sound that you could hear

was the spoon

rattling 'round my Daddy's coffee cup.

My Daddy looked like Jimmy Cagney

small and quick

I had to trot to match his pace.

He loved to laugh, my Dad.

And his ready grin had crinkles carved

at the corners of his hazel eyes.

What was left of his hair was parted down the centre

and his zest for life

spanned the fault lines of what was and what is.

Where has he gone?

Where have they gone?

Those times, those people

those places I loved?

Away.

Far away.

'Our Town' is but a memory anymore

the cottonwoods watch empty streets

abandoned buildings.

The Halcyon days, the store, my Daddy,

away.

Beyond the knee deep Maple

beyond the Alice Slough

beyond the Badlands in the Westernesse

farther

forever farther

than sundown.

Magic Carpet

The cash machine in our store
had a metal plate on the cowling,
'National Cash Register'
embossed upon it.
Built sixty years
before they changed the name to 'NCR'
that old machine was huge.
Four foot wide or thereabouts
it weighed three hundred pounds
if it weighed an ounce.

There were four big drawers
with numbers on 'em
When I was five
my Daddy hit a button wrong
and a drawer popped out
hit me in the forehead
knocked me on my bum
like a pole axed steer.

Those drawers were really heavy

solid oak they were.

I kept an eye out after that.

There's a shelf above the drawers

with a sheet of milk white glass on top.

It's where our Daddy's

coffee cup and ash tray used to set.

Almost sixty years it's been

and in a flash of used to be

here's my Daddy

standing next to me

his almost trademark

Alice Fairway apron

with it's strings

wrapped around his front

and tied.

He's got a cup of coffee in his hand

and held between the fingers on the other

the burning cigarette he was rarely seen without.

The button panel on our register

curved away and up

from the milk white shelf

and had about a million keys.

Only two of which

were mostly ever used

the one you punch

to pick the drawer you want

and the one to open it up.

When you hit that open key

you could feel the motor running.

The big old fly wheel spinning

and the rumble whirr clatter thunk

when the drive gear tripped

and threw the cash drawer open.

For all the world

it sounded like an Owatana Baler tying knots.

My Momma sold that register

after Daddy died

in nineteen sixty-nine.

and I haven't heard it's sound

in nearly fifty years.

But once in every little while,

I get a hint

that brings that cash machine

screaming to my mind.

A sound thats hidden

almost out of sight

like it's trying to disguise itself.

The first time ever that I heard

the wheels inside a slot machine

go thunk

I saw my Daddy standing there

at our ancient register

ever present coffee cup in his hand

his finger on the key.

I think I actually felt the drive wheel jump

there in the eye of my mind

when it opened up that oaken drawer.

Some folks think

a picture filled photo album

is the best and only link

to that which went before.

There's no use in my denying it

I love to look at pictures too.

But the things that really free

the Magic Carpet in my mind

are the sounds and smells

that link me

to those things and people

that had an impact on my life.

An Owatana baler tying knots.

A slot machine going thunk.

The tinkle of a spoon in a coffee cup.

Or the thoughts

risen from the ashes

by the smoke of a burning cigarette.

Left to themselves

they don't mean a thing.

But when they hit that key

and the drawer slides open

in my heart,

and my Dad walks by

trailing wisps of cigarette.

It's then I know for sure

that it's the sounds and the smells

that truly are the power source

for the Magic Carpet of my mind.

Uncle Ernie's Bee House

'Bout a mile south of town

a little ways north of Alice Slough

there's a building used to stand

sat there off the highway twenty, thirty, rods

High pitched roof, wooden shingles

gray

Nothing really set it off.

It just sat in silhouette,

against the western sky

If you made that turn off the highway though

headed up the drive thats somehow longer than it looks

that curls around and down

a little prairie hollow filled with willow brush

before heading up the roll where the building sat.

Along the way that building somehow seemed to grow

to half again the size you thought it was

My Uncle Ernie owned the place

for long as I remember

And I don't know if it had a special name

We just called it

Uncle Ernie's Bee House.

See back in nineteen twenty-one or twenty-two

when Maple Valley Gardens was shiny new.

You remember Maple Valley Gardens?

Those Maple Valley Strawberries

and the biggest apple orchard

for a hundred miles around?

Well the story goes

my Uncle Ernie

was eating honey toast for breakfast

when he happened to happen to read the label

on that honey jar.

Saw it came from an apiary

down in Iowa

No thunder roll no lightning flash

he just decided there and then

if it was good enough for Iowa

it was prolly a whole lot better

for a Bohunk from Dakotah.

The Bee House was a special place for me

going up that drive

through the hollow filled with willow brush

and up the prairie roll to where the building sat.

The Bee House sat there silent mostly

Kind of stark and lonely looking in it's grayness

Except each fall of course

when the canning happened

The humming of the centrifuge

the clinking clatter of a thousand mason jars

the clanging din of fifty pound silver tins

like stacks of empty jerry cans

You could even taste it on your tongue

the golden sweetness of the honey

in the very air

Over fifty years in our little corner of existence

Ernie and his bee house were to honey

what Kellogg's is to corn flakes

In the nineteen fifties nothing else came even close

It wasn't pasteurized, homogenized, or adulterated

It wasn't blended, blanched, beaten or churned

It was just as it came from the comb it was

Some was nearly clear

delicate and airy as a Dakotah breeze in June

Some, had the almost smoky glow of ancient amber

A hint of peat from Alice Slough

There's a hundred golden shades

"Bohunk" was originally a term of contempt, referring to an unskilled none too bright person of Bohemian extraction. Uncle Ernie was obviously being self deprecating in its' use. By the time I was a boy in the fifties it had become a term used when one had done something less than brilliant. So rather than call a person stupid for an error he'd be called a Bohunk to take some of the sting out of the rebuke. I don't think I've heard the term used outside of my hometown of Alice, ND

to Uncle Ernie's honey

the subtlety of a hundred magic flavors

And if you thought about it for a minute

you could even taste the prairie's soul

'Bout a mile south of town

a little ways north of Alice Slough

there's a building used to stand

sat there off the highway twenty, thirty, rods

High pitched roof, wooden shingles

gray

Nothing really set it off

it just sat in silhouette

against the western sky

Our family Christmas gift from Uncle Ernie

came from there every year

A fifty pound polished silver tin

of the same sweet golden treasure every time.

And every one so unique

in color, hue and subtlety of flavor

In a world that doesn't know

or has forgotten what is genuine

one thing truly stays the same

when swirled around on the tongue.

There's a complex taste

separates the fiction from the truth

a taste thats missed a lot these days I think

the savory sweet of being real.

Tapestry

Have I ever told you

about how the plate glass windows of our store

are a time machine for me?

It hasn't been a "Fairway Foods"

for half a century and more

but I can put my face against the glass

shield my eyes with both my hands

and watch the Alice Fairway calendar on the wall

the one we gave away at Christmas time

change its month and day and year

to whenever fancy takes me.

It's nineteen fifty two behind that glass right now

and I am there leaning on the candy case

bibs of faded corduroy

neck to navel zipper in the front

I got a Pluto picture on my t-shirt

leather high top farmer shoes

and my hands are held behind my back listening to the talk

My Momma's words that children should be seen

and never ever heard

coursing through my mind

Beneath the milk white globe

of the single light

that hangs up there over top the furnace grate

a group of guys sit on slatted benches

talking politics and baseball

and other grown up stuff.

Old Ezra's there leaning on the counter

he's the one that calls me 'Zip'

On account of the zipper in my bibs

Ezra chews a lot of snoose

that dribbles down the corners of his chin

and when he talks he sounds like Gabby Hayes

Ezra's farm was on the way to Grampa's place

only just an open field there now

where his house and barn

and twenty acre grove used to be

"snoose' is a colloquialism for snuff, it and the brand name "Copenhagen" were used interchangeably.

Big Russ is holding court today

his heavy frame stretched out

ankles resting on a crate that's meant for eggs.

His twelve ounce Pepsi Cola bottle loosely gripped

propped against his big old belly

every inch of which is bought and paid for

so he says

Russell is an expert

on anything you ever heard of

and a whole lot probably that you haven't

Thats the way it sounds at any rate

to hear him talk

If there's a thing that he's not sure o

it's for sure he'd not admit it.

And then again if Russell drops the verbal ball

Frankie's there to pick it up and run with it

When either one is at a loss

they sort of act as seconds for each other

in the never ending game of words

Frankie used to run the Farmer's Grain

he never was formally accused I guess

for those years the books had failed to balance.

Now he mows the grass in our town

has a riding mower we kids think is great

'cause most of us still mow by hand

When Frankie's out there mowing

he wears a hat thats really cool

my Daddy told me it's a Pith Helmet

and I thought that he was saying something nasty

till I saw the movie 'Gunga Din'

Frankie was a lot like Russ

though he might not have a clue about it

he'd talk on any subject under the sun

My Daddy said

'If you gave old Frankie half an inch'

He'd try to drive an NP locomotive through it

Frankie's favorite thing though

to talk about

without a doubt was baseball.

And until the team for Alice finally folded

He'd been an Alice Angel almost forty years

After twenty four losing seasons

consecutive

the Angels finally called it quits

when only two men showed for practice

in the spring of nineteen fifty two

Frankie, who'd been pitcher over thirty years

and a younger fella named Duane

who probably hadn't heard about the losing streak.

The other players said they had to quit

twenty four losing seasons was bad enough

but to take the chance of it becoming twenty five

to take the chance on a 'Quarter Century' losing streak

was way too horrible to comprehend.

So anyway when Frankie starts on baseball

My Daddy says 'He'd lay me odds'

it's going to finally come around

to the last time that

the Angels had a winning season

nineteen-hundred twenty-seven

That's the year that Frankie pitched

that almost nearly shut out

in the playoff game

against the mighty Indie's

of Enderlin, North Dakotah.

A game at night it was

the only lighted park

for a hundred miles around was Hendrickson

the park the Indie's call their home.

The score was tied nothing all

in the bottom of the tenth

when the Indie's center fielder Carl Lindeman

stepped up to the plate

They called old Carl 'Cottonwood'

And it wasn't hard to figure

why they named him for a tree

him being six foot six and all.

I don't know for sure how heavy Cottonwood was

but they say they had to weigh him

at the Cargill Feed And Seed

on a scale they use for grain.

It was the fifth at bat for Cottonwood

Frankie'd struck him out each time before

when he swung so hard

at Frankie's change up pitch

people said it looked like Cottonwood

would screw himself in the ground.

There was a big typhoon

in the Dutch East Indies

a week or so following the game.

The swags at the 'Friendly Sticks'

the pool hall down in Enderlin

allowed as how the wind from Carl's bat

might have been a factor in that storm

from the Butterfly effect and all.

So there it was

the bottom of the tenth.

Maybe Frankie got complacent

having struck old Carl out

in four at bats that night

or maybe Frankie just got tired.

Frankie says old Cottonwood got plain dumb lucky.

When he hit that change up pitch so hard

he whacked the cover right off the ball

broke the light out from the tower

above the fence in centre field.

The longest homer ever

in the history of Hendrickson field.

A teacher at the high school was heard to say

if it hadn't hit the light

it would have gone

five hundred feet and more

Some of the 'Boys' in the stands

sharing a brew... or two.... or three...or nine

Home brew it was a'course, it being prohibition and all

Some of those 'Boys' allowed

as to how they doubted

that ball would'a ever landed at all

on account of it was still going up

when it hit the light.

Yeah Frankie still talks

about how lucky old Cottonwood was

a quarter century ago.

And as I peer through all the dimness

of fifty years of window glass

At the five year old leaning on the candy case that's me.

I see and hear and smell,

Those sights and sounds and odors,

That he takes for granted in his world.

The nutty brown aroma of percolating coffee

from the stainless steel urn

on the counter by his shoulder.

Up in the room where Daddy tests the farmers cream

the cloying sour sharpness of acid burned butter fat.

There's oiled leather work boots in a glassed in case up front

that smelled like walking in a room

with a hundred brand new baseball mitts.

Jet black overshoes so high they need five buckles

And vinegar that drips beneath the barrel bung out back

so that I can almost taste my Gramma's German Dills.

There's a great huge burlap bag

filled with peanuts salted in the shell.

When you stick your hand in there

cast around for a nut

it makes a sound like walking through dry leaves in the fall.

I'm no philosopher nor even very smart

given all the errors I've made throughout my life.

But I think we all of us have a window

where everything thats happened

to me or you or anyone

is there behind the glass.

Those happenings are the threads

woven in the fabric of our lives

Each one looked at separately doesn't count for very much

But woven all together

to become the sum and total of who and what we are

those threads don't make a simple fabric

They make the precious tapestries

that decorate the corridors of the keeps that are our lives.

Snippets of Their Lives

Next door across the alley

from our store to the North

was Angeline's cafe

and next to that

Emil's Hardware store

Angeline's closed it's doors for good

in nineteen fifty nine

and Emil's then

in sixty four or five.

And there used to be a shop

across the street to the west

sold implements, equipment for the farm.

The building walls

were sided with

that silver painted tin

stamped to look like bricks.

For near a hundred years

people scratched their names

and messages

upon those walls.

Wrote snippets of their lives

in our Dakota town.

Names and messages

forgotten mostly anymore

like the wall

that they were written on

as if they'd never been at all.

A Norman Rockwell Painting

The "Have a Seat"

the barber shop in my home town

reminded me of a Norman Rockwell painting.

Even though the building's gone those many years ago

I feel its' essence still.

I see it there

with the "Minneapolis Moline" dealership

next door to the South

and Corcoran's Auto Shop to the North

I see it just as clearly now as then.

Old Swit the barber standing by the window

scissors in his hand

the kind that has that little hook

by the finger hole.

Old Swit is standing there

behind the barber chair

cutting uncle Eddy's hair.

I always thought

that barber chair was super special

arms of porcelain, buttons out of brass.

The leather pads of the rounded seat and oval back

burnished bright from a million pairs of overalls.

And there's a lever on the side of stainless steel

that Swit would use to raise the chair for shorter guys

lower it for tall.

The footrest on that chair a work of art

a polished stainless filigree of moulded leaves and flowers.

And of course I can't forget

the leather razor strop

that hung there from the arm

seems like it always swayed a little

like a pendulum in the sun.

There's an old pot belly in the corner

kept the shop nice and warm fifty years.

Some folks tried to talk

Old Swit to switch to propane

But like he said

'been workin' fine for near on sixty years

an if it ain't broke no sense in tryin' to fix it.'

I can see a couple fellas through the window glass

waiting on those oak and leather couches

with the cuspidors at either end.

Magazines and papers strewn about

Life and Look and a hundred kinds

of farmer rancher stuff.

Not a one of which is less than 2 years old.

And mounted there above the mirror

the antelope and nine point buck

Sylvester shot in nineteen twenty-six.

So vivid are my memories

almost I feel that I can touch them.

I think that it's the hundred thousand scents and smells

and barber shop aromas that trigger me.

The leather of the couches and the chairs

the Red Oil polished wood and sixty years of smoke

from all those cigarettes and cigars

And what about that green concoction

Sylvester dipped his comb in?

Smelled to me

like lying in a flower bed

in the middle of a lightning storm.

But you know what?

Mostly it's that hair oil smell

that creamy-oily Wild Root hair oil smell

that made it feel like I was part

of a Norman Rockwell painting.

Ode to a Ballpark

Four blocks from our store

to the west and south

was the ball park where we used to play

The bases and home plate are gone

forgotten in a box somewhere

upstairs in some garage.

And that canvas sack

of wooden bats?

I can feel the one I used to use

the Louisville Slugger

with the quarter inch chip in the handle

in my hands as I write this

There hasn't been a ballgame there

in half a century

where I used to could

in the long ago

hit a baseball past

the plum tree rows

beyond the center field.

The pitcher's mound
where my brother used to throw
is hidden anymore
by prairie grass up to our thighs.
I never had an arm like him
but I stood there on the rubber
once or twice
pretending.

Those plum trees though
that formed the outfield line
where we'd go to get a snack
in between the innings
still are there.
And the posts
that held the chicken wire
that caught the balls going foul
those greyed out posts
stick up
like a line of naked trees
leaning at an angle
from a hundred years of wind
across my Northern Steppe.

I know it doesn't look

much like it anymore

but this place was a ballpark

in the long ago.

and day by day

with the pass of time

fewer folks remember.

Won't be all that long

and there'll be no one left

to talk about this field that was

here in my hometown

in the long ago.

The Genuine Article

It was in the nineteen fifties that I learned

that home cured sausage, German franks, and Bohemian Smoked Ham

didn't come off an assembly line

if they truly were

the genuine article.

Walking through the door

I always had the feeling

I was stepping through

the portals of a cave

It was probably the echo made it feel that way

Stangler's Butcher Shop

was the only place in my home town made of stone

A'course it wasn't stone for real

It was great big bricks done up brown and rough

like in Boston and New York.

The windows in the front

are high up on the wall

and there's a single bulb for light

hanging from the ceiling

A pull string eight foot long about

works the switch to turn it on

The light was always sorta dim in there

on account'a Mr. Stangler

used the lowest wattage

he could find

The dimness and the echo

made me feel a need to whisper

like there was a force I couldn't see

compelling me to quiet and decorum.

A dichotomy of sorts that force.

Cuz if you talked

even just to say hello

you could feel the sound bouncing off the walls

and in your ears

for what seemed

like forever.

The colors in the shop

were like a pair of jeans washed too many times

thin

faded near to nothingness.

Even bright red steaks behind the glass in the cooler

looked dusty rose in their pans of porcelain.

And the air of Stangler's Butcher Shop

had a taste and smell

like sucking on a copper penny

with an ice pick up my nose.

Like my Gramma

cooking up a batch of homemade soap

with renderings and lye.

The thing that dominated though

was the smokehouse out in back

Applewood and hickory

honey, salt and vinegar

brown sugar and a bunch'a spices most folks never heard of

and I think 'ol Butch

might'a even used

beer and bourbon whiskey.

Back in the nineteen thirties

Stangler's Meats were famous.

Northern Plains Bohemian Smoked Ham .

(the recipe a closely guarded secret)

Those hams were shipped

to movie stars and gentry

'round the world .

The likes of Loretta Young and Jimmy Cagney

Bette Davis and Pat O'Brian

and even Maurice Chevalier

got their holiday smoked ham

from Stangler's Market

Alice , North Dakota

USA

The story goes

that in the latter nineteen thirties

"Butch" was shipping out

five hundred hams at Christmas time

Three four hundred more at Easter

Things were going well for "Butch"

So well he thought about

Bohemian Smoked Turkeys

for Thanksgiving

He never got around to turkeys though

Outside forces contrived to end his enterprise

'Ol Butch was heard to say in later years

"Yah I heard dat he vass Catholic "

"But at least dat Gott damn Hitler "

"vass not Bohemian"

Stangler's kinda lost a step during the war

and the shop was never quite the same after that.

By the latter nineteen forties

a shadow of its' former self

Oh the smokehouse kept on going right enough

but never ever came even close

to the salad days of the nineteen thirties

By the time that Mr. Stangler died in nineteen-sixty-two

the shop was more a hobby than a business enterprise

and since he took his recipes

with him to the grave

his family decided

to simply close the doors.

The building sat there empty over thirty years

then in nineteen ninety four or five someone knocked it down

for the rustic brownstone bricks

Just weeds and broken glass anymore

where I learned

Stangler's home cured sausage

German Franks and Bohemian Smoked Ham

truly were

the genuine article.

Flower Gardens and Lightning Storms

I remember when I started school.

I can put my finger on the spot

where Momma used to part my hair when she combed it.

It's on the left

three inches up about from my ear.

She'd wet it down

and comb it forward first

then put the Wave Set

on that big green comb

put it on my part.

and pull my hair to the right

then comb it down and to the left.

I can feel that comb

as if it were right now

smell the Wave Set fresh and light

like a flower garden

in a lightning storm.

Our old school was the tallest building in our town

if you didn't count the elevators

down by the N.P. tracks.

It only had two stories

but the twelve foot ceilings

really added to the height.

They were covered with

those copper sheets

stamped with vines and flowers

so in vogue

when the century was young

fifty years of paint though

flattened the effect a bit.

Pictures of the Presidents

Washington and Lincoln

and the Ten Commandments in gothic script

hung from wires fastened to the molding

up along the ceiling.

They leaned out

a little from the wall

propped up top like they were

on the blackboards there.

Even as a little kid

I knew a lot of people

had used those black slate boards.

I felt like I was carrying on tradition

like I was in

a guild of ancient scribes

when I wrote my lessons there.

Now I don't want to say

the windows in my school were loose

but the glass would rattle

and the sash weights in the frames

would jump and thump

every time there was a breeze.

And in the wintertime

when that prairie wind was blowing

snowdrifts would appear

on those ten inch window sills.

The windows in my school

were huge

four foot wide

and eight foot tall about

and most all the light we read by came from them.

There was a cabinet of mahogany

hung up top the blackboard on the wall

had world maps hung like window shades inside

from when this was a high school years ago

You used a wooden rod

to pull them down to see

It was fun to look at what the world was like

thirty years before ever I was born

The wooden desks in my old school

looked like polished amber

so in the sun in afternoon they seemed to glow.

And the frames were iron filigree

that swirled and flowed

like ivy on a trellis

you could always tell which desk was mine

by that patch of scratched off varnish on the seat-back

where my suspender buckles rubbed.

Our old school was built

when people mostly still trusted in each other

We didn't have no private lockers and the like

Two rows of hooks on the wall sufficed

an upper one for older kids

another closer to the floor

for little ones like me.

And the row of overshoes beneath the coats

lined like soldiers at attention.

A Red Wing pot was the water cooler

with a porcelain bowl attached

and a button that you pressed

to get a drink.

There's a hundred things

about my school that come to mind.

The woody perfume smell

of cedar shavings

from a million sharpened pencils.

The chalky white of erasers

in a thousand youthful hands

wiping clean those black-slate boards.

And in the wintertime

the copper taste of steam

in thumping radiators.

Their sizzle was the music in the background

of our classroom symphony.

And too there was the smell

like a flock of sheep caught in the rain

twenty sets of woolen mittens

roasting on the radiator.

They'd get so hard

we had to pound them on the brick foundation

to make them soft again.

They tore down my old school

the summer I was nine

built a new one nice and modern.

I don't know what happened

to the bell we'd been so used to

they replaced it though

with something that they said was better

a new electric buzzer.

At the time

I didn't know the word nostalgia

that I'd miss that old bell

and a bunch of other things.

Oh I like that we've got indoor plumbing now

that we don't have to go outside when it's thirty-five below

but I didn't realize it then

that we always pay somehow

for so called progress.

It's for sure that I don't have

all the answers

I got lots of questions mostly.

I sometimes wonder

if the price we pay isn't way too high.

When I get lost and need a place to flee to

I hope that I recall

the fresh clean scent

of flower gardens in lightning storms.

The Box of Glass

I was searching for the means

by which to erase

a desperate bit of doggerel I had writ.

When instead I found an other thing

in the stationery drawer

of that ancient roll-top desk.

I found it there not secreted

enshrined I think a better word

in a smallish box of glass and polished brass.

Though I hadn't seen it's like in sixty years

from the moment I espied it

I knew that I beheld a relic

took me to a gentler time

more civilized some would say, than now.

For it was you see, a flower

not one you might expect

to be preserved and pressed between the pages

of an heirloom book.

Rather it was from

a Mother's day six decades past.

And I must confess that it's existence

had escaped my memory

until I found it there

not secreted

in a smallish box of glass and polished brass.

For it was a white carnation

crafted by my hand of seven years.

A kleenex tissue torn and frayed and fluffed

fastened by a bobby pin

and worn as boutonnière

those years ago.

And in a smallish box of glass and polished brass

she had kept it

from a Mothers Day six decades past

a time more civilized some would say than now.

It was in fact the actual Kleenex carnation I had made for mom when I was in grade two. She kept most every Christmas, Valentine, and especially Mother's Day thing we kids had done for her, had it all secreted, "enshrined" out of sight. And it's only now, since she's lost a step or two, that we're discovering that hoard.

Back Behind The Butcher Shop

We didn't have a rink
in our town when we were young.
We skated on that pond
back behind the butcher shop.
A swampy slough in summertime
it wasn't very smooth for skating on
on account'a the water
flowed in constantly
from that Artesian well
back there.
If you didn't know
where the really rough spots were
you could crack up good.
A friend of mine
when we were eight
he fell and broke a tooth
right out of his head.
That ring of cattails 'round the place
gave a little shelter from the wind.

But I'm here to tell you

toes get really cold

at thirty five below

cattail ring or not.

We kids would never

come right out and say it

but that pond

was kind of ugly in the daylight

on account'a

all the minerals in the water

made the ice a yellow green.

Sort of like the runoff

from a cow barn when it's froze.

But at night

when the Northern Lights were running wild

the total opposite was true

and I know that pond wasn't holy

but it seemed almost to glow those times

like what you'd think

something sanctified would do.

The Artesian well went dry

sometime in the eighties

the butcher shop got razed

in nineteen ninety five or so.

You'd never recognize

the spot we used to skate.

My sister told me recently

how back when she was just a girl

after I'd left home for school.

Like us boys used to do

she'd take a shovel

made for scooping grain

scrape the snow from the ice

back there on that pond.

She'd work so hard she said

that when the job was done

she'd lotta times

be too tired to skate.

I wish that I'da known

she skated there a half a century ago.

I maybe could have joined her

and then I'd have a memory

of her and I skating on that pond that is no more

back behind the butcher shop

in that then of long ago.

Cottonwood Dreams

On the corner back behind our house

where the street goes past the Alice Hall

down by the front of Emile Blasel's place.

In the corner of that open field back there

there lived a great huge cottonwood.

Biggest one I'd ever seen.

Five of us hand in hand couldn't reach around it.

I love cottonwoods.

Living on the prairie where trees are pretty scarce

I treasure every one.

But that old girl on the corner was my favorite

darned few trees choose to live

up there on the prairie where the grass is tall.

They mostly choose the river bottoms

or get planted close where people live.

By the time that I was nine

I knew most every tree

for miles around my home town

And even though I love them all

it's the native born

that are really sort of special.

It's why I loved that cottonwood I guess

it wasn't planted by some person

it sprouted wild by itself in the middle of the grass.

Waxing tall and strong on her own.

That cottonwood was here

before my town was even thought of.

Already past it's teens

when my house was being built.

The rough cork bark is thickened now

great deep fissures etched into it's sides

from eighty years of winter on the northern plains.

It's leafy canopy is iridescent green

and in the prairie breeze

its waxy leaves flash a heliograph to God.

I took for granted when I was nine

what I thought that everybody knew

that trees and people talk.

Those trees they whisper

in a language I can only feel

that resonates deep inside my core.

I used to climb that tree near every day

Forty feet or so from the ground

there's a spot where two limbs branch apart

like a giant slingshot crotch

It became a great huge easy chair

custom made for me

where I could sit and watch the world

embraced up there by my tree.

Some people call it imagining

Some people call it dreaming

I'd sit up there in my easy chair

close my eyes so that I could see

And I would see pictures of my town

of a minute ago or half a century past

Like the day I looked

and right in front of church was parked a car

wooden spokes and curtains on the sides

worn out shoes and empty cans hanging from the bumper

"Love and Happiness Joe and Ida"

whitewashed on the doors.

My Gramma and my Grandpa on their wedding day

in nineteen hundred sixteen.

And of course I can't forget the time I saw my Momma

ten years old or thereabouts and pretty as a picture

her hair is in a twenties bob

and in that hat she's wearing looks like Clara Boe

The thing I really notice though

is that clear eyed gaze of hers

is it looking straight at me?

Is it my imagining or does she really see

through the tapestry of time?

The scenes I seem to see

are like pictures in a stereopticon

through a window on the past

I blink my eyes and there's the Alice Mercantile

With three four cars and a couple horse drawn rigs out front

A block away the old NP

snorts and smokes and spews hot steam

and four doors down just past the hardware store

the livery stable and hotel.

My Grandpa said they both burned down

before we went to war in nineteen-hundred seventeen.

I'd never seen an early picture of my town

And didn't till my Gramma passed in sixty five

In her memory box we found a penny postcard

a picture of Main Street in my hometown in nineteen-hundred twelve

The livery stable and hotel were there

and I got goosebumps when I saw it

cause that picture is identical

to that dream that whispered in my mind

in a language I could only feel

high atop my cottonwood

when I was nine.

You Could Say that it's a Miracle

The village hall in Alice, North Dakota

looks better than I would have thought

after all this time.

When I look around and see

how the rest of my home town has fared

you could almost say that it's a miracle.

The painted white three inch lap

looks good.

The windows are intact

and I see the town replaced

those worn out double doors

out front.

It's really nothing special

our village hall.

Just a box a hundred foot or so in length.

The shallow angle of the roof

allows a ceiling height of twenty feet

on account of we played basketball in there.

At the end farthest from the entrance door

there's a stage Art Deco trimmed

in deep red stained mahogany.

Christmas plays and movies

Smokers for the Wildlife Club

and bands for every dance

held in town for sixty years played that stage.

At age thirteen I even got to see

Bobby Vee and his Shadow's play.

The windows on the sides are eight foot tall

and the floor is solid maple

with a parquet circle in the centre

W.P.A.

ALICE, N.D

1934

inlaid in the wood.

My Momma was a high school girl when it got built

by the Works Progress Administration

One of Franklin D's New Deal projects

in the Great Depression.

She likes to tell the story

how before the hall was there

the only way she saw a movie ever

was sitting in the grass

behind the firetruck garage.

On summer Saturdays

they'd stretch a bedsheet out

between two trees

and the whole darned town

turned out beneath the stars

to watch the picture show.

The movie cost four cents

a penny for the popcorn

a nickel went a long, long ways

in that used to be.

The school in my hometown

never had an auditorium

for sports and plays and things

or programs for the holidays

And before the hall was built

the only dances thereabouts

were in barns or sheds

or outdoors on the street.

As soon as it was built

that hall was special to my town

with all the memories

of dances and matriculations

programs, plays, and holiday festivities

even roller skating

on a Friday night.

It's only natural I suppose

for special things to stand out in my mind

I remember carnivals

and costume parties at Halloween

and paper bags of candy

at the holidays.

And I especially remember

that I was the elf in the Christmas play

when I was in grade three.

And I remember shooting paper wads

over top the canvas curtain

that kept the grades apart

when we had our classes in the Alice Hall

while the brand new Alice school was being built.

To remember a couple dozen moments

special times in my life

really doesn't do it justice.

I know our Alice Hall

in the great and grand scheme of things

was pretty unimportant to the world.

But to the people living there.

There in my Dakota town

it occupied a niche

near the center of our world.

With the school and church

it gave a little focus to our lives.

That old Hall

is the only thing remaining

of that time.

The Alice school became a senior center

forty years ago

And even that got closed up recently

for lack of clientele.

Probably the hardest thing

for my town

was when Saint Henry's church

according to the Bishop

had so few parishioners

that it "wasn't viable economically."

So they shut it down a few years back

what they called

'Diocesan Consolidation '

The Alice Hall

survives today

looks better than I would have thought

after all this time.

And though they have to marry somewhere else these days

It still gets used from time to time

for wedding dances and the like.

You could almost say that it's a miracle.

Rainbows and Recollections

Did you ever stop to really think

about the little things that pop to mind

when you're steeped within a recollection?

Sometimes

when I'm aware enough to pay attention

I surprise myself with what I see.

Like the other day

when I heard a man

talking about guns in schools.

I had a picture in my mind

just that quick of my old school

The one that they tore down when I was nine.

And like someone opened up a door

I was there in that then

where being safe was furthest from our minds.

Guns and violence were for us

like people in the tropics

they might hear about that frigid weather

and those blizzards way up north

but it was still impossible

for them to fully comprehend

what it really meant.

Blizzard was just another word to them.

And I was vaulted to my school.

I could hear the creaking of the boards

smell the wax upon the gleaming floors

I could see the sun

reflected from those dished out spots

those shallow hollows

worn into the steps of the stairs

There's an echo too

seems to amplify itself

when voices bounce off ceilings

twelve foot overhead

I could feel the windows rattle in the wind

smell the wet wool smell of mittens

drying on the radiator

And as I sit here trying

to find the words to describe

what chalk dust does inside my nose

I can see the world is edgier today

its' angles sharper to the eye.

I recall the curves back then

that felt so comforting

Like the woodwork at my school

that I would swear was warm to the touch.

And I think about

how the window glass was flawed.

How it warped and bent and split

So that when the sun came shining through

the colors of the rainbow

splashed across the Maple floor.

And I think about

how a rainbow's mostly what I'd rather see

than guns in schools and such

when I'm steeped within a recollection.

Saint Henry's on The Plains

There was nothing very special about Saint Henry's.

Just a little prairie church

in a little prairie town.

It's churchliness perhaps

the least of its' identity.

See Saint Henry's was the loom

that wove the fabric of our world.

Saint Henry's was the thing unchanging in our lives

a place of safety and tradition we could flee to

wrap around us like a cloak and cowl.

So instilled in me was that sense

that when I see a church today

be it onion dome in Russia

or stupa in Nepal

I smell the beeswax candles

of Saint Henry's on the plains.

Time stood mostly still

in our prairie town

so insulated from the world.

So when they ripped the heart and soul

from that place.

Closed down our little prairie church.

They tore the very fabric of our lives.

Just a threadbare tapestry

of memories anymore

of beeswax candles

and Saint Henry's on the plains

I'm quite aware that the closing of Saint Henry's was not the cause of the demise of my hometown. Having said that, having grown up in a town of 100 people give or take, of whom 99% were Catholic, the church was the epicenter of our lives. It's closing did, I believe, greatly accelerate a process probably already irreversible .

Midnight Masses and May Crownings

Did you ever notice

how the incense lays in ambush

for the mustiness and damp

creeping up the stairs

from the basement?

Or the way

it's ancient scent

conjures in your mind

marble floors, stately columns

and cut glass windows

honoring the Virgin and the Saints?

Did you ever notice

how a cough reverberates...

bounces off the nave

in the stillness?

Or how

the Holy water basin

builds a crust around the edges

so that when you dip your finger tips

you feel the grit?

Did you ever notice

those scruffy little tufts of hair

sprouting from the ears

of the old man in the pew ahead?

Or thought of how

they look like suckers

growing at the corners

of your Gramma's porch?

Did you ever see a mother

struggling to calm her child

having finally to succumb

and scurry off

to the quiet room.

Did you ever wonder

if that too loud alto in the choir

always half-a-step off key

really thinks

the music's

writ that way?

Did you ever let

that special shade of green

pull you like a lodestone through the years

to the Christmas crèche

on the Joseph side of church?

And did you ever wonder

how just the smell of beeswax candles

could bring us back

to

Midnight Masses and May Crownings?

*At Saint Henry's Catholic church in
my hometown there were three
statues, one of Saint Henry out in
the vestibule, and one each of Mary
and Joseph down front on pedestals
on either side of the church . So I in
my mind labeled the church with
Mary and Joseph sides rather than
right and left*

Memorial Day

I thought I was alone

out there at the cemetery.

The ceremony thirty minutes done

I'd tarried there awhile

waited till, I thought, everyone had gone

to snatch a bit of time

out of time

in solitude.

Even in a crowd anymore

I'm oftentimes alone.

My camera lens, my pad and paper

my thoughts and memories

my companions.

In those times

of solitude and reflection

the world somehow

comes in sharper focus.

Time seems eager

to loose it's hold

on reality.

I thought I was alone

at the cemetery

when I found him in my camera lens

His head was bowed

he didn't see me there

eighty yards away.

And I felt my muscles twitch

my hand remembering

the clutch and release

of his move from bead to bead

on the Rosary

dangling from his fingertips

That Rosary seemed somehow to form a bridge

between the was and is

With the camera and its' telephoto lens

held against my eye

we had an anonymous communion he and I

There

in that prairie cemetery

where for a moment

time had loosed its' hold

on reality

Saint Henry's Picnic 1961

I had my growth

that summer nineteen sixty-one.

Took after Grandpa Joe they said

Strong as a bull they said

Pretty much indestructible they said

And I could hit a baseball

they used to say

nigh on a country mile

So it was summer

nineteen hundred sixty-one

Sunday

Saint Henry's annual picnic Sunday

Free popcorn

a dozen kinds of potato salad

and pickles

A hundred kinds of pickles

Chicken from my folks's store batter fried

and home cured German sausages

from Stangler's Meats down the block

Sunday.

Saint Henry's annual picnic Sunday.

The Sunday of the annual softball game

the men against the boys.

At the end of summer

the year before.

The end of summer nineteen sixty

Clarence and his family

had moved to town to run the Standard Oil.

See Clarence had married an Alice girl.

Met her out in California during the War

lived out there fifteen years or so

after he mustered out.

They had four boys Evelyn and Clarence

Rangy boys

tall

athletic.

Great additions to our softball team.

And at Saint Henry's picnic softball game

the men against the boys

the boys had always beat the men

At least as long

as anyone alive could recall

or would care to talk about.

I'd heard some stories though

'bout when Alice, North Dakota

was a baseball town for real

back in the teens and twenties.

But that was forty years before

'bout how the men every year

would beat the the boys unmercifully.

Not much chance of that

happening this year though

'Cause we boys were really, really good.

And after all

they used to say

I could hit a baseball

nigh on a country mile.

We won the toss that day we boys

so we were first to bat.

And when we talked it over

we decided

we'd intimidate and demoralize our Dads

right off from the start.

So I'd lead off

'cause they used to say

I could hit a baseball

nigh on a country mile.

Mr. Kemmer was the catcher for the men that day.

He ran the Standard Farm Delivery Service.

Everybody called him just Duane mostly.

'ol Duane had a voice pitched way up high.

My Momma used to say

he chattered like a magpie.

Tall and lanky

with a dozen knees and elbows

he looked kinda like a human spider

crouched down there behind home plate.

He could'a been a jester at a court

in another time and place

so the rapid fire repartee of a catcher

came naturally to 'ol Duane.

So I'm the first one up to bat.

And I'm walking to the plate

my favorite bat is in my hand

it's a Hillerich and Bradsby

my good 'ol H&B.

A lot of people used to wonder why

I didn't use a Louisville Slugger bat

like so many other guys.

So I'd just say 'the proof is in the swingin''

and after all

they used to say

I could hit a baseball

nigh on a country mile.

So I'm walking to the plate

and I'm just a little puzzled

'cause there's 'ol Clarence

tall and skinny grey haired Clarence.

Clarence, who must be

thirty eight or nine if he's a day

standing on the pitchers mound.

And I stop outside the batters box

prop my bat against my thigh

as I grab a dusty handful

of the prairie earth

to dry the perspiration from my palms.

And I contemplate the situation

and I can hear 'ol Duane with his catcher's repartee

yelling batterbatterbatter,

as the umpire yells 'batter up.'

And I look out there to the pitchers mound

where old Clarence stands

not nearly nervous

as I think that he should be

facing me

the big strong kid

the kid they used to say

could hit a baseball

nigh on a country mile.

So I take my stance

in the batters box

and I can hear 'ol Duane

with his catchers repartee

and there stands Clarence

decidedly relaxed.

I can see the flash of white

of the brand new softball in his glove.

And when I think upon it

back upon that day

I should'a known

that there was something fishy going on.

'Cause most of us used baseball gloves.

Just a little under sized

to hold a softball comfortably.

But that big old glove that Clarence had

looked as if it might be made

especially for a softball

'cause that ball fit so well inside of it

it almost disappeared.

So I'm watching him

and he slowly reaches with his arm

across his body

to grasp the softball in his glove.

Then he looks on down towards me

nods his head at old Duane

just a little nod

like you see the big league pitchers do.

And I'm standing there in my crouch

behind me 'ol Duane and his banter

that clutters up the air.

And I see 'ol Clarence straighten up

and it sorta looks as if

he arches back his upper body just a bit.

And he takes a big deep breath

lets it out with a whoosh

that I can hear

from all the way down here

at home plate.

His right arm starts to move

and his left leg comes up off the ground.

I don't really think that Clarence

had ever heard

of Quantum Physics

Universes Parallel and such

but his left foot

the one attached to the leg thats in the air up off the ground

threw up clouds of dust when it landed in the dirt

the very instant that I heard

the softball strike

'ol Duane's catcher's mitt.

I never saw the ball.

I never saw the doggone ball leave his hand.

I thought I must have had a seizure

or a narcoleptic fit or some damn thing.

'Cause I never saw the ball in the air.

He must have pitched it though

'cause there it was

in 'ol Duane's catcher's mitt.

And the umpire yelled 'Steeerike One'.

Loud.

And I was way embarrassed

lookin' 'round for a hole to crawl into.

Then 'ol Duane tossed the ball back to Clarence

on the pitchers mound.

So I settled in

gritted hard my teeth.

Prepared my mind for the second pitch.

After all

they used to say

I could hit a baseball

nigh on a country mile.

I saw the ball this time thank God.

But I think I might'a been

paralyzed or something.

'Cause it pounded all the dust

out of 'ol Duane's catcher's mitt

before I had a chance to swing.

And the umpire yelled 'Steeerike Two'

really loud

and here's the kid

who people used to say

could hit a baseball

nigh on a country mile

down 0 & two in the count

and he hasn't even swung his bat.

So I determined there and then

that I'd anticipate old Clarence

beat him to the punch I figured.

So I settled in.

Got myself all psyched.

And when I saw him

getting close to the end

of his big 'ol windmill windup

I began my swing.

I knew my bat would get there

at the same time as the ball

but what I didn't know at the time

was that 'ol Duane the catcher

had signaled out to Clarence

to have him throw a change up pitch.

I think I could'a swung three times

before that ball floated to the plate

I could almost swear

that softball gave to me

a raspberry as it floated by

about a half an hour

after I'd already swung.

So the big strong kid.

Strong as a bull they used to say.

The one they used to say

could hit a baseball

nigh on a country mile.

Well.

I damned near screwed myself into the ground

swinging at that pitch.

So we boys lost to the men

twenty three to zip that day.

Saint Henry's picnic Sunday

nineteen sixty-one.

And I guess if there's a thought

I carry with me from that day

It's this:

though you think you may be able

to hit a baseball

nigh on a country mile

never underestimate

the grey haired guy on the pitchers mound.

Found out later that "old" Clarence
had pitched semi-pro softball out in
California for ten years after he'd
mustered out of the Navy at the end of
World War II, a fact his kids had been
sworn to secrecy about so as not to
warn us boys. Not that it would have
made any difference, I can honestly say
I've never seen a pitcher before or since
do the things with a softball that
"old"Clarence did.

Persepolis

When I walk my town today

When I look beyond the obvious

It occurs to me that with the pass of years

it crossed a threshold of a sort.

The razed and empty spaces there

the picked clean bones of that that was.

Where once the streets were lined with trees

gone feral lilacs lie like winged lions

along the rubbled byways of my personal Persepolis

And those phalanxes of cottonwoods

the gymnasiums of my youth

strewn and scattered like some Attic ruin.

When I walk my town today

it occurs to me

that I'm an archaeologist of a sort

sifting through the detritus

of the razed and empty spaces there

the picked clean bones of that that was.

Victim of The Times

They took away the track

of the old NP yesterday.

Prized it up

from that century old right-of-way.

A victim of the times they said.

They took away the track I walked a thousand times

from the Farmers Grain

to the cut out there

a half a mile away

through the prairie roll

We'd be cowboys there in summer time

dig snow-caves in the drifts

when it was cold.

They took away the track

of the old NP yesterday.

The track I used to balance on

to see how far that I could walk without tipping

stepping on the cinders and the clinkers

left over from the steam-trains years ago.

They took away the track

of the old NP yesterday

another item on the list

gone missing from my prairie town

A victim of the times

they said.

Prairie Whispers

I surprise myself sometimes

at the things my mind

seems to find important.

Though I have to say

when I climb behind my eyes and look around

those memories of my Northern Plains

are mostly what I see.

So I guess I can't be held at fault too over much

for telling you whats really there

Sure there's other things

in the landscape of my mind

but truth be known

they don't seem to matter over much.

At this moment frozen in my dream

the thing that resonates for me

is that open field behind our store.

I'm standing there

and right in front of me

that marshy area where all those ducks and mud hens

nest in summertime.

and there's about a million pheasants too

in the grassland just beyond.

Most folks think of chickens

when they hear of roosters morning calls

but when I grew up it was pheasants

crowing at the dawn.

There's a four foot terra cotta culvert

goes beneath the NP tracks over to my right

where the marshy area smacks against the grade

And excepting for the spring time

when the melt is on

it's mostly high and dry

the ends obscured by tumbleweeds and such.

On any given day that old culvert

is the Catacombs of Rome or the Fortress of Bastille

or any of a half a hundred other places

our imaginations take us.

The railroad tracks are twelve foot up

from the surface of the marsh.

An elevated track

'cause the old NP needs a level bed

on which to run its trains.

That high line grade is really steep

like climbing up a mountain.

'Cause when the crews laid the rails

they didn't care to make the landscape pretty

they just did what they were hired to do

make the road bed level and make it true.

And because that grade is so steep

when you finally get up closer to the top

your nose is level with the tracks.

And you notice all the smells

at once repulsive and compelling.

The low note of the creosote

mixed with oil and tar and stuff.

And hiding there almost out of sight

like a never ending high note

from a far away piano

the acrid stink of diesel fuel poorly burnt.

I didn't walk the tracks as much in summertime

'cause I was going barefoot mostly.

And there were lots of cinders strewn about.

Refugees from a generation past

and the bygone days of steam.

They say the cinders in the roadbed

kept the weeds from growing.

It's for sure that they were hard on my bare feet.

I sort of love to hate the train

With its' rumble and its' stink.

Like a snoring dinosaur with halitosis.

Even at the age of ten

I marched a little out of step with the world.

I preferred the almost silence of the prairie

the distant murmur of the cottonwoods

the silken swish of thigh high grass

swirling in the summer breeze.

If you stand with me

by that open field behind our store

by that marsh that smacks against the NP tracks

close your eyes and listen

you too will hear

hear my prairie whisper in your ear.

The Very Stones

There's a thing they do in movies

to show the passing time.

You barely blink your eyes

and a person, place or thing

fades and disappears

like a candle flame

snuffed out in a prairie wind.

The world is like that too I think

we know instinctively within our minds

that there is nothing permanent or real.

That everything we've ever known

will finally fade and disappear.

Yet in our hearts

we still believe as children do

that there are things

unchanging as the very stones.

That cottonwood I used to call my own

the big one that I always climbed

sat in by the hour.

It seemed as if

only but a moment passed

since I had turned away.

Where had been

its' leaves of iridescent green

that shimmered in the sun

a pile of wood chips now.

I recall so clearly

across the alley from our store

Angeline's cafe and the hardware store one door past

tumbleweeds and broken glass anymore.

where once they stood

a Wild Prairie Rose has taken root

in the crack between the sidewalk and foundation

blooms there in the dirt

like a post apocalyptic scene

from Dresden or Berlin.

How from the ashes of what was

life will rise again.

I turned around one day

and the railroad train I loved to hate

with its' noise and diesel stink

had disappeared.

The emptiness I felt

like a winter wind

blowing through the hole

its' passing left within my soul.

I recall the words

from a song of years ago.

Turn around and you're one

Turn around and you're four

Turn around and you're a young man

Going out of my door.

It's about the changes happening

in the seeming wink of an eye

to those people, places and things I loved.

I sometimes wonder

is their aura only there for me?

I think that they are lodestones

of a secret kind

that draw me magically

to the memories of the things I loved.

To that place within my heart

where I can still

believe as children do

that there are things unchanging as the very stones.

Sanctuary

I was sittin' here the other day
thinkin'
'Bout how I usta' go
a mile or so north of town
to Clemmie Heinz's place
to snare a bunch'a gophers in his pasture.
Not a lotta people know about
snarin' gophers.
That it was a dying art
when I was twelve
and I'd even make so bold to say
the art is more n' likely dead today.
So remember when I talked about
that big ol' pail
Christmas candy used to come in
at our store?
Made of metal painted grey.
Thing about it was it had a lid
with a buncha' little ears around the edge
for to re-attach it if you wanted to.
And it had a bail too with wooden handle
made it nice for to carry.
I could snare a gopher

stick it in the pail

put the lid back on.

But wait a second here

here I am

gophers in the pail

before they're even snared

and thats the art of it

the snarin' part

can't forget the snarin' part.

See whatchya' do is get some cord

that skinny yellow braided kind

they use for layin' out foundations.

You get a piece kinda long

'bout fifteen feet or so

and tie a loop at the end.

Then ya feed the cord through the loop

and make it like a lariat

then settle in and watch.

Ya settle in and watch those gophers

stick their little heads up

stick 'em out from their holes

and bark and call.

And you walk a little closer

and when the gopher ducks his head

you watch which hole that he went down.

When you get close

those gophers dive back down their holes

hide underground.

And you take that braided yellow cord

make a loop like a lariat

lay it down

'round the outside edge

of that gopher hole.

You take the other end of that cord

and sit and wait.

See gophers are

really curious little critters

as soon as it gets quiet

that curiosity is like to bust 'em open.

They seem compelled

by forces uncontrollable

to stick their little heads up

take a look

see what's goin' on

look to see if you're up there still.

You'll only see his nose at first

stickin' up to test the air

to see if he could smell you

sittin' there very still and quiet

down wind from the hole

out of sight pretty much.

He'll pull back down for half a second

and then his head'll pop back up again,

little eyes of polished onyx.

And fifteen seconds later
his shoulders start to rise above the rim
and you jerk the cord, pull it tight.
And where just a second in the past
all was calm and quiet
with a curious little gopher
tryin' to look around
now you've got a critter gone berserk
and fightin' mad on the end of your cord
like a salmon fighting current.
And you haul him over
bouncing on the end of the line
like that salmon on a hook
drop him in the pail.
When his weight is off the cord
it slackens up, slips right off.
And even though the sides of the pail
for climbing are too slippery
you lay the cover on it anyway .
In an hour of a summer afternoon
you can snare ten or twelve
of the little critters.
I made sure I didn't hurt 'em though
Cuz I always let 'em go when I was done .
I don't recall for sure when Clemmie died ,
a couple years after I left home I think .
The folks that bought his place

had no truck with cows.

So they broke that prairie pasture to the plow.

And when they did

the gophers there

just up and disappeared.

Never saw their like around here after that.

Later on I got to thinkin' some

'bout what happened to the little critters.

And I think I maybe got it figured out.

See I don't think those guys were gophers after all.

See Prairie Dogs used to live

all over North Dakota

and there's still a bunch of them where there's lots of grass.

But they don't care so much for cultivated ground

so as the land went under plow they moved out further west.

Clemmie's pasture wasn't broke 'til nineteen sixty eight.

It had been a sanctuary eighty years

for those Prairie Dogs.

Kinda like my Grampa's farm

was for me.

An island sanctuary

In the Prairie Sea.

The Farm

Grandpa's Pipe Smoke

Cathedral bells and anvils

No two sound alike I think

And it's the one that sits there

on that tree stump sunk three foot

in the floor of Grandpa's shop

that rings through time for me.

Sixty years and counting

since last that anvil rang.

It's sound still lingers in the doorway of my mind.

And if you should ask

'Why is it unique?'

I doubt that I could answer.

I'd shift my feet and stammer

stare out the window

say something stupid

like it has a sound that sneaks inside

wraps itself around my bones I guess.

Some folks say I'm weird that way

how I remember stuff

the forge, the bellows

the tongs and smithing tools.

The first thing though

that you notice

do you smell that high note?

Sixty years of sparrows

roosted in the rafters

spent their lives up there.

Half a century idle

and that leather harness

hanging from the pegs on the center post

still bears the hoary rime of draft horse sweat.

And of course the prairie wind

has dropped a load of dust

on everything.

Repurposed tins full of odds and ends

lie in no apparent order atop the bench.

Hess's Udder Balm holds nuts and bolts and washers

Hanson's Harness Dressing filled with nails

and in the Velvet can a thousand flathead screws

their purpose long forgotten.

On the wall above the bench an ancient calendar hangs

forever December nineteen hundred eleven

a faded picture of joyous children

cherubic smiles extolling the virtues

of Pear's Perfumed Soap

half a century hence.

My Grandad was a powerful man.

You always knew when he was working

from the measured strokes on the anvil

and the pipe smoke in the air.

Some folks say that I'm a little weird

the way that I remember stuff.

Over sixty years since last that anvil rang

it must have snuck inside

wrapped itself around my bones I guess

'cause I will swear that I can smell

my Grandpa's pipe smoke on the air.

Feed Bin Door

The charcoal marks seem almost to glow.

Incendiary runes

of a century past

when he burned the letters of his name

into the feed bin door.

Sparrows in the loft

go boisterously about their lives

to the sound of cottonwoods

whispering a hundred feet away

and the scents of

dusty hay and old manure

grow fainter

year by passing year.

There's a sense of lonely here

a sweetly bitter after taste

of hind sight from the century past.

And all thats left to mark his passage

are the letters of his name

burned into the feed bin door.

Seventy Seasons Past

Year by passing year my drivers sink

inches deeper in the prairie sod

and I wait.

I wait and ruminate

the yoke of time

heavy on my rusted shoulders.

Seventy seasons

since last I breathed

a chaff strewn breeze

since last I belched hot steam

reveled in the heat.

And I wait.

Seventy seasons

since last my heart pulsed and surged

glowed red.

Since my drive belt

flapped and slapped

ebbed and flowed

slack and taut

when the spikers dropped their bundles

An anthropomorphic soliloquy by my Grandfather's 20 ton Avery steam tractor that was obsoleted in 1949 by an Alis Chalmers machine fueled by gasoline.

in the gleaners open throat.

And I wait

I wait for the seething heaving

liquid stroke of the shaft

that drives my 20 ton bulk.

For polished fittings

gleaming in the prairie sun.

Patena'd petcocks

that sizzle and drip

under my fiery belly.

And I wait.

For the bundle stiffs

the water monkeys

my engineer

can of oil like a long neck bird

in his hand

poking its' beak

in all my parts.

And my goggled fireman

stuffing my fiery belly

with sunlight colored straw.

And heat.

Heat that blisters a face

that leans too close to my heart.

Heat that turns the wheels of what I am.

And what I am is what I was

seventy seasons past.

If machines have souls

mine was left

on a chaff strewn breeze

there in the sun

there in the dust

there in the heat

seventy seasons past.

A steam threshing operation would have driven OSHA personnel to drink. The drive wheel for the heavy canvas drive belt that stretched out for perhaps a hundred feet had no cowling, the belt just flapped and slapped in the wind, moving as much as three or four feet up and down, woe betide the unwary whose shirt sleeve or glove got caught in the wheel or belt, men were known to lose fingers and even arms. The spikers and bundle stiffs, the men who tossed tied bundles of grain from the shocks (where they had been propped up teepee style to dry for several days) to a wagon and then transported them to the waiting threshing rig or gleaner. Straw was burned to keep the steam up on the tractor. It burned very hot but needed to be constantly tended as it also burned very quickly. The water monkey kept the boiler replenished, and the engineer oversaw the steamer operation. It took roughly 20 men to properly run a threshing operation.

Harvest Song

It used to hang up there

opposite the tulip window

up above the fabric fern

that sat for fifty years

on that stand of stained mahogany.

That photo of the harvest scene.

That picture of the threshing rigs

and tractors run by steam.

Remember when the sun

shone through those cut glass

tulips?

Lit that old brown tone

with a greenish yellow light?

It made that picture come alive for me

like I could climb inside that photograph

hear the harness bells

the clinking of the chains

as great huge horses drew their wagons near.

The window in the foyer of Uncle Ernie's house was a round leaded glass window of yellow tulips, that, in the afternoon would fill the foyer with a lovely light. The photograph was typical of the era , perhaps a foot high and two and a half feet wide, depicting an entire threshing operation with a wide angle lens.

And the light would shimmer in the waves of heat

rolling off the twelve foot steamers

like rollers off a windy sea.

I could smell the sweat and grease and grime

of goggled men with three-tined forks

stoking boilers up to temp with straw.

The steam from those machines

a mist as from a super heated geyser.

And the twelve inch canvas belts

that stretched two hundred feet

slapped and flapped and sang

like the drawn tight stays of a clipper ship racing under sail.

And the threshing rig

the gleaner with its' bourdon whine

that set my very bones aquiver.

The breathless wheezing hiss of the steamers

The nickers and the neighs

and shouts and whistles of the horses and the crew.

A kind of order

borne of chaos and confusion

dissonance controlled in a symphony of sorts.

I am grateful that a hundred years and counting

since that photograph was done

when I look into it's depths

I am grateful the symphony still sounds for me.

Peeking Through the Prairie Grass

In the yard is where it lay

the wheel barrow.

Lays there on it's side

in the lawn grass overgrown

encroached upon more and more

every year by the wild.

Pansies and Petunia's cascaded down

in that other then.

Spilt their colored blooms

on the carpet there that was the lawn.

Built by hand a hundred years ago

my Granddad fashioned it,

out of angle iron and pipe.

Planks that were a grain tank once

are the box.

And in the front

a two foot packer wheel,

purloined from a pony drill.

Twenty years that wheel barrow

hauled grain and feed

and garden plants and flower pots

and when the chicken coop got cleaned,

it carried all that fertilizer

down the hill to the garden.

But as the decade of the twenties waned,

pretty much retired it was,

to mostly lighter chores.

There came a day in summer though,

in nineteen twenty, eight or nine.

My Mom was nine or ten,

and her little sis my aunt Lorraine

seven or eight or so.

Pepper and salt they were

those little girls.

My fair and freckled mom

and my aunt Lorraine

the color of a chocolate malt

in the prairie sun.

Those two had a special bond

that went beyond the blood

that's lasted ninety years.

So on this day in summer

in nineteen twenty, eight or nine

it was decided by those girls

to help their Daddy with a chore.

See their Momma said she wanted

to have a flower bed

ten foot from the Chinese Elm

just North of center in the yard

And she needed prairie loam

for to fill the bed that she had planned.

Five barrow loads of loam

their Daddy hauled that day.

He filled a sixth at supper time

left it for the morning.

The girls decided there and then

to help their Daddy out.

Surprise him.

Have that wheel barrow full of loam

emptied in the flower bed

when Daddy got there in the morning.

None of us were there to see of course

how hard they worked

those little girls.

To go two hundred yards

with a loaded wheel barrow

that they got to where they did

tells more than words about them.

It's why that barrow

lies there yet today on it's side

about ten foot from the Chinese Elm

just North of center in the yard

It's why their Dad and Momma left it there.

A shrine of sorts they said

to girls of enterprise, feeling and ambition

They planted flowers in it every year you see

in the loam that spilt upon the ground.

It lays there yet today

the wheel barrow.

Nearly hidden in the grass.

As the prairie year by year

takes back a little more of its' own.

And though it's been some ninety years

if you come back in summer time.

you can see sometimes

yet today on that barrow spill

a pansy or petunia

peeking through the prairie grass

"pony drill" I tried to find the definition in a number of sources and for the life of me couldn't find any reference to the term. It was however in common use when I was a boy. It referred to a drill (seeder) just a few feet wide designed to be pulled behind another implement such as a plow or cultivator. It allowed the farmer to perform two operations in one pass over the ground. ie: cultivating and seeding.

The Photograph

I don't recall a time it wasn't there

hanging from that wire

on the parlour wall

I don't recall a time

I wasn't drawn to it.

The oval frame

with it's glass gently curved

gave testimony to the age

of the photograph within

Ostrich plumes and imitation flowers

decorate the twelve inch brim

on the ladies' hat

There's a bustle in her floor length skirt

and her lacy blouse

is done in needle point with tiny roses

and pearls the size of mustard seeds.

A countryfied Gibson Girl

from a previous century

The fellow seated there in front of her

wears glasses rimmed with wire

and his upper lip

seems to almost not exist

hidden by the mustache there

He has a breadth of shoulder

that hints of underlying strength

and every bit the gentleman he looks

with that pearl necktie pin

waistcoat out of silk

and the bowler in his lap.

The lady isn't tall

but stands there ramrod straight

her hand upon the shoulder of the man

the both of them

focused on the camera lens

their clear grey eyes riveted it seems

on me

almost as if to send a message

from the then to the now.

I ask myself

if someone in a century or so

will contemplate my picture.

Ask the questions I have asked.

Wonder who the fellow was

in that photograph

on a future parlour wall.

Hollow Sound

It was a hollow sound

a hollow scraping sound

that grabbed me up

set me down in that then.

A then when butter melted on the plate

and the smell of fried bologna

filled the air.

When parsnips browned in bacon fat

lay golden in the pan.

And a loaf of fresh baked bread

waited on the sideboard to be sliced.

On the radio you could hear

the price of grain in Minneapolis.

And the screen door slapped a couple times

like it does when someone comes or goes.

And the chair at the table head

as it became occupied

creaked

squeaked a little

scraped the hardwood floor

with a hollow sound.

Winter Afternoons

When the temperature is low enough

to let zero seem a heat wave

it's with a fondness

I recall winter afternoons at the farm.

It's when the little sounds in the quiet there

seem louder

and the smells and scents

to which little heed is mostly paid

are sharper and more salient.

When the swinging of the pendulum

in the clock above the sideboard

is contrapuntal

with the tick, tick, tick of the cooling stove

and the coffee smells

from the white enamel pot

tickle at my nose.

It's the way the pages of Dakotah Farmer

rustle when my Grandpa turns them

or the velvety tobacco smoke

from the pipe that he is puffing on.

If I close my eyes today

cock my head just so

I can hear his fingernails

drumming on the table top

smell the fried bologna and the sauerkraut

Grandma made for dinner.

When the temperature is low enough

to let zero seem a heat wave

on those winter afternoons

at the farm.

Thigh High Grass

For long as I remember

I've wished that they could talk.

The stories they could tell

those machines.

Those nearly forgotten

obsolete machines.

Thigh high grass the color of dry sand

surrounds me.

And names.

Names etched in steel and wood and rust.

Names that roll from the tongue

almost like family.

Like McCormick and Deere and Case.

Runes really

relics of a nearly forgotten past

There is no plastic here.

No gleaming chrome or aluminum

Only steel.

Steel and wood

and the rust of course

the rust.

Like that single furrow horse drawn plow.

Dull and lifeless now

oaken handles rotting.

They still shine where he gripped them though

oil and sweat steeped in the wood keeps it new I guess.

And see that tractor there?

The one on which I sat my Grandpa's lap?

The seat that shined with an OshKosh glow in that then

dull and pitted now.

And over there

the rusted carcass of that giant Avery Steamer.

Forty years fire and smoke

belched from its' twenty ton maw.

Silent now

these four score and counting

giant wheels sunk a foot or more

in the prairie sod.

And see the harrow handle jutting skyward?

its' silhouette

looks like the head of some exotic bird

in a trick of light in the late day sun.

Like those shadow creatures

we projected on our bedroom walls

when we were young.

I remember as a little boy

thinking that the thrashing rig

was a monster that we had to feed.

I got a shiver every time

a bundle got consumed.

The relief I felt

that it wasn't me.

That gleaner hasn't moved since nineteen forty nine

I hadn't yet gone three when it was obsoleted.

I played for many years around that rusty rig

pretending I was Grandpa

running a threshing crew.

If you look behind that threshing rig

you'll see the Chevy

partly hidden in the grass.

My Uncle Ernie got the dealership

in nineteen thirty four.

Ernie, Uncle Frank, and my Grandpa

the only ones bought cars that year.

Thirty four the middle of Hard Times and all.

Their cars were all the same

forest green, suicide doors, dual fender wells,

tear drop headlights made of chrome

and mohair seats so sharp

they looked like gangster cars from Chicago.

Ernie dropped the dealership in nineteen thirty five

just wanted to get a car on the cheap he said.

My Grandpa used to take me fishing in that chevy

down to the knee deep Maple.

It wasn't about the fishing though

he and I together was what it was.

I can see him as I write this

his image conjured

by the burnt tobacco smell that lingers there

and though it's been twenty years and nine

since it was driven

there's flecks from his cigar stuck there still

where he spit 'em on the dash.

And the butt of a William Penn in the tray.

There's a sickle mower with a clam shell seat

in that taller grass behind the car

right where its been since nineteen fifty two

the last time Grandpa cut the hay.

And the last of the horses too

died that year.

Frank was a Clyde

and Bob the last of the Percheron's

Pretty much pets

the last ten years or so

they'd been around since the early nineteen twenties.

Methuselah's for horses

that didn't keep me from missing them though.

And fifty two was also the year that Barney died

I really missed that old dog.

I guess that you could say

Bob and Frank and Barney

got obsoleted too.

My Momma used to tell me

I ate like I worked on a threshing crew.

And I got to thinking about those

threshing crews

'cause when she was a girl

it took twenty men

to work a threshing rig

Today the job is done by two.

And I thought about that

gleaner and that steamer

and so many machines

obsoleted.

And a question comes to mind

that I really have to ask.

How long will it be

before I'm obsoleted?

How long will it be

before I'm parked over

in the thigh high grass?

An Old and Trusted Friend

Every time I look in it's direction

those empty window frames

like a pair of staring eyes

are looking back at me.

It was at first unnerving

so much did I feel

that there truly is a presence there.

It turned a hundred ten a couple years ago

that falling down clapboard shack

three rods or so from the barn.

In spite of age

and weathered look

it has a certain regal air about it.

The kind of air accorded Doctors of Philosophy

in threadbare Irish tweeds

with patches on their elbows.

For reasons that I really

don't fully understand

when that old place comes to mind

*a "Rod" is a 16 1/2 foot
unit of length. When my
Grandad grew up the term
was in general use but
over time fell out of favor
except in the surveying
profession. I use the term
simply because he used it
a lot in his conversations
and it seems to make him,
for me, more present in
my writing.*

148

the picture that I always see

is sepia toned.

See it's where my Momma's Daddy lived

his first years in Dakotah

when as he was wont to say

when he was 'batchin' it.'

"Batchin' it... when Grandpa
was living alone, as a bachelor

When he lived there all alone

before my Gramma Ida

came upon the scene.

My Granddad only had

a fourth grade education

but the fifteen prairie winters

he spent there in that shack

gave him time to study and to read

instilled a love of knowledge

just for the sake of it.

Which he in turn

gave to his girls

and now has passed to me.

So when I see that old place

those willow shoots

jutting through the vacant window frames

like the eyebrows on an English teacher I once had.

I feel a kind of kinship

with that weathered shack

like an old and trusted friend.

Haymow Door

Went to see the farm the other day

don't remember last I'd been.

Thought perhaps the pass of time

might have rounded off the edges just a bit

of my powers to recall.

Been standing there

a hundred years and more

that once red barn

Greyed-out umber now

a century of prairie wind and sun

takes a toll.

The roofs' caved in on the lean

where my momma and her sisters used to milk

and the haymow door

hanging on its hinges

leaves a gaping hole there in front

from a broken latch

there's no one left to fix.

And when I stood there looking

that prairie wind blowing down my neck

when I saw that haymow door

slapping in the breeze

I saw my Grandad of a Sunday

in his rumpled suit

with that short wide tie

that was the fashion of the day

three quarter century ago.

The way that tie would flap and slap

in the wind

the way that haymow door

slaps and bangs today.

I Wish That They Could Talk

I used to wonder at

the thickness of his fingers

bigger than my wrists it seemed.

The nails too had a look

almost patina about them

Like weathered wooden shingles

silvered by the prairie wind and sun.

Even in his eighties my Grandpa's hands

were hard as field stone

and soft as kitten's fur

in a moment of caress

They're a kind of metaphor those hands.

To a life where even scars have memories.

Like that one two inches long

between his finger and his thumb.

Even eighty years ago

skinning knives were sharp.

And that patch of white on his fingertips?

Too many times frozen

in the winter wind.

There are craters too in that leathery hide

drips of smithy metal gone astray.

And eighty years of prairie sun and wind

left a shade of brown that never fades.

Sometimes I wish his hands could talk

and I'd have had a tape recorder.

Cause so many of the thoughts

from my beginning times

have those hands inside of them.

When he and I would walk

it didn't really matter over much

where we two were going

when I could feel his hand

wrapped around my own.

I felt sometimes as if

it was my Grandpa's grasp

kept me in the here and now,

helped to ground me in the world.

I sometimes wish his hands could talk

and I'd have had a tape recorder.

Sunday Supper At The Farm

Sunday afternoon

Thirty eight below

So cold the snow

no longer scrunches when you walk

more like it squeaks

like a hinge on a rusty gate.

The sky is that hard enamel blue of winter

and a watery yellow late day sun

pushes the long blue shadows of December

across the drifted prairie

I can't feel my toes.

I got on Rockford socks in my high-top shoes

and overshoes that buckle to my knee

and it's so cold I can't feel my toes.

Daddy and Momma are in the front with baby Mary.

Me and Darrel my little brother are here in the back.

We're going to the farm for Sunday supper.

I stand behind my Daddy looking out the front

cause it's the only window in the car

that isn't frosted over.

I take my mitten off and with my fingernails and warm breath

on the window to my left

open a gap in the frost

Sucking on my frost numbed fingertips

I peer through that opening

like I'm looking through the eyepiece of a periscope.

I can see Ezra Krueger's place

so there's only three more miles to go!

The road we're on is a one lane gravel section line

covered up with snow

and when our car hits a drift

it bucks and rattles

like ramming a frozen railroad tie

and the gear box whines

like a diving B-29

as it labors through the pillow drifts

that cross the township road

And there!

The ker-flumping of the planks

on the bridge across the knee deep Maple.

Just a mile and a half to go.

When we get there to the farm

the sun looks like

a glowing copper ingot

sitting on the world's edge.

We troop into the house

as a shaft of light from that blood-red sun

pierces through the nearly dark

the beveled glass of the kitchen cupboard doors catching and reflecting it

and the room is filled with a honey glow.

that seems to pulse

with a light that's all it's own.

A moment only it lingers

then fades with the setting sun.

The thing you notice first in Gramma's kitchen

is how cozy warm it is.

Coats and mittens and scarves

get piled by the kitchen door

and the old cook stove seems to beckon you

to warm up in its' glow.

The table there in Grandma's kitchen

has room enough for eight

but I remember many more

sitting there for Christmas or Thanksgiving.

A oil cloth the same shape as the table

protects the top from damage

and when my Grandpa drums his nails

it makes a sound like a woodpecker

drumming a hundred yards away.

The chairs are nothing special

there in Gramma's kitchen

twenty coats of varnish black

and wooden spokes for the backs.

There's an undertone too

in that kitchen

of the burning wood in the old cook stove.

It's not so much that you always notice it

it's just that it's 'there' if you deign to pay attention.

I think sometimes the kitchen smells

are pressed into the very walls.

And when Gramma fries the parsnips, sausage and sauerkraut

it just frees aroma's up

from those already there.

Else how could those smells

be so deep in my brain

unless they were there all the time?

For Christmas this year

Grandpa and Grandma got a tv.

We don't have one at home.

So while Momma and Grandma

finish the supper

Daddy and Grandpa and Darrel and I

get to watch.

I wonder if the lady on the screen

really can see me.

Cause Daddy and Grandpa keep teasing

telling me that she can.

She's real pretty and always seems to be smiling

I wonder ... is she really smiling at me?

It's pitch dark outside about five o-clock

when Gramma says it's supper time.

The meals are always served

in the pans that they were cooked in.

A cast iron skillet for the parsnips and potatoes.

Another for the sausages and sauerkraut.

I and Darrel are too small

to lift the heavy pans

so Momma fills our plates.

And when everybody's ready

Grandpa says the Grace.

Seeing his hands folded in prayer

always had an effect on me.

It shifted something deep inside

something in my heart I think.

To see those great thick fingers

humbly make the sign of the Cross ...

then intertwine in supplication

those moments

those moments frozen in time

they weren't just a moments for God

my Grandpa knew

they were moments for family too.

Like a hundred other moments

that conjure up these memories.

Why the smell of a stove or burning wood

can bring tears to my eyes today

Or that lump that forms in my throat

when someone says the Grace

Those moments on which

I vault through time

to that place where family is

To that place where still

I'm having Sunday supper at the farm.

He Walked in Kindness

He was six foot tall in his prime

shrank a little over time

as gravity took its' long term toll.

But you wouldn't have noticed his height so much

as the breadth of his chest and shoulders.

I have snippets of memory

dreams almost

lying nestled in the crook of a massive arm

My rump being held in a palm overlarge

by great thick fingers

on gentle and powerful hands.

Hands like dark tanned leather

stretched over a frame of iron and oak.

Hands of a smith forging hot steel.

A farmers hands birthing foals

or harnessing a four horse team.

A fathers hands never raised in anger.

My Grandpa's face was ruddy

seventy years of wind across the drift.

His eyes the same clear blue as my Mom's

had crinkles at the corners

three quarter century of laughter

and squinting at the prairie sun.

He wears his hide a little looser anymore

wattles kind of jiggle when he laughs

leans forward some when he walks

bucking a prairie wind from force of habit.

Like pacing on the deck of a clipper ship

there's a definite roll to his step.

He wore a plaid wool cap

flaps pulled down in the cold

and a tattered straw in summertime

I never saw him in dungarees

I don't think he even owned a pair.

Oshkosh bibs

with their clips and buttons of brass

his answer to fashion on the farm.

There's probably a hundred things

that bring his image to my mind

the spicy smell of fresh sawn wood

an anvil sounding like a ringing bell

the creak of the rocker he rocked me in

or the way his slippers hissed

when they slid across the polished maple floors.

But guaranteed to set my tears to flowing

the Prince Albert smell of an ancient briarwood pipe.

When my mom and aunts say Dad

the word slides slowly

off the tongue

like they're somehow tasting it

savoring it's flavor.

To them it's not just 'Dad'

Dad is way too small a word

to convey the depth of feeling that they have.

It really isn't a word to them

like 'Grandpa' isn't a word to me.

What it really is,

is a loving caress in disguise

I never heard him raise his voice

or use a four letter word.

He wasn't famous or even very important

Just a quiet and honest man

who loved his family and his God.

I remember a line from Byron

that's stayed with me.

'She walks in beauty like the night'

With my apologies to Byron

It brings my Grandpa to my mind,

he walked in kindness in the light.

We Just Spell It Differently

I think that it's about

a hundred below outside

and the light's so bright from the sun on the snow

when I go back in the house

everything white glows pink and fuzzy.

I think I might have froze my face off

helping Grandpa do the chores

cause' it sure feels good here in the kitchen

next to Gramma's stove.

Bob and Frank are really old

so Grandpa feeds them extra hay and oats

just to help keep them warm.

My job is getting all the eggs

out from under the hens.

Grampa's hands are so big

the chickens always peck him.

Not that he seems to mind so much

his hands are really tough.

I got small ones though

that slip right under

so the chickens hardly know I'm there.

I was scared at first

to put my hand down there

I didn't wanna get pecked.

But that was long ago

when I was four.

Four whole days till Christmas.

I can hardly wait.

And my birthday's three days later

and I'll be six this year.

We're having milk toast, Grandpa and me.

Grandpa says to warm our bones after chores.

Milk toast never tastes so good

as here in Gramma's kitchen.

Gramma says it's nothing special.

Just toast from home baked bread

in pieces in a bowl

with cinnamon sugar and hot milk poured on top.

We sometimes have it at my house

but it never tastes as good as it does right here.

Here in Gramma's kitchen.

It's four o-clock or there abouts
and it'll soon be dark.
The sun is red
looks like a copper penny sitting there
on the west horizon.
I was sitting at the kitchen table
finishing my toast when I saw it,
through the beveled glass
of the kitchen cupboard doors
the living room just started to glow.
with a golden light through the window bay.
Grandpa saw me looking
looking at the light exploding in the room.

Grandpa makes a sound sometimes,
That's not a laugh and not a chuckle.
It sounds a little like a nicker
that the horses make.
He seems to make it when
He thinks there is a question
that I maybe ought to ask

and he doesn't want to come right out and tell me.

So I asked about the light

so golden in the living room

and he began to talk.

At first I didn't understand

he talked about a place so far away

a place in Britain they call Stonehenge.

No one knows for sure

who built the thing he said.

A great stone circle

set up to track the sun.

And on winter solstice, twenty one December

the sun shines through, between two stones,

and lights the centre with a golden glow.

Those people long ago thought the sun was God you see.

Grandpa surely never planned it

but the way he built the house and shop.

The way they line up with the sun.

On twenty one December does the sun

shine right through the stained glass window bay,

With a golden almost Holy light.

Grandpa says he's not a Druid or anything like that.

But he thinks

we're more alike than different.

His prairie Stonehenge rather proves it to him.

He says he figures

We're like those people of

long ago Great Britain.

We just spell "Son" differently.

Pickled Beets and Bottle Rockets

I can hear the clack of wooden balls and mallets

from the croquet game going on

beyond the open window.

Across the way the hum-chitta-thunk

of the stanchion pump

keeping the water tank cold

to chill the pop and beer.

It's Fourth of July at the farm.

I swing my legs under the chair

nursing my glass of Kool-aid

wondering how

I could'a been so dumb

Grandpa was poison in croquet

and I was the first one that he hit.

Doesn't really matter though

as soon as Momma makes the salad

we're gonna play kitten ball in the yard.

A Seven-up sign is home plate

squashed flat coffee cans the bases

over the granary or into the trees

an automatic out

It's really hot inside the kitchen

a hundred degrees, maybe more

and Gramma just pulled the rhubarb pies from the oven

Their tart tangy smell

sets my mouth to watering

so awful much I have to swallow a couple times

just to keep from drowning.

Gramma's facing away from me

working at the range

I can feel her watching though

with that set of eyes I can't see.

I hear a voice that sounds like hers

but I'm pretty sure it belongs to God

"If you think you're getting a slice of pie

you're sadly mistaken young man

so get outside and play kitten-ball with the others ".

Gramma has a way of saying stuff like that

so to make you feel totally guilty

just for wishing...

I love rhubarb pie.

And I loved our family picnics at the farm

Aunt Mildred usually so dignified

laughing like a girl.

Aunt Lorraine like a cruise director

on an ocean going liner

so concerned that everyone has fun.

My Daddy

cigarette stuck between his teeth

he would have had a coffee cup

but he needs both hands to bat.

Uncle Mac doesn't play kitten-ball

cause he gave a lung to T.B.

but we couldn't play the game

without his teasing and his jokes.

Everyone gets to play

from the youngest to the oldest

Even Grandpa gets to swing the bat

but he has a pinch runner

he says he's too old for that.

After the game it's supper time.

There's about a hundred kinds of food

at picnics at the farm

fresh hot buns, home cured ham

Gramma's potato salad with lots of onions and mustard

and wild horseradish to give it that extra punch.

We have burgers and dogs

batter dipped chicken fried in lard

and there's a million kinds of pickles

all of em' home canned.

Sweet and sour and everything in between

my favorites are Bohemian Dills

and my Gramma's pickled beets.

It's fireworks and bottle rockets after supper for the kids

and at dusk my Daddy does the Roman candles.

It's almost like it was rehearsed somehow

he sticks the rocket in the ground

then lights it with his cigarette

and runs to get away

we all go OOOOO and AHHHHH and clap

when it lights the prairie sky.

Kids would more than likely say today

eewww how boring or some such thing.

I guess I never realized

how unsophisticated we were

we were like some nineteen forties movie

or a Norman Rockwell painting.

To tell the honest truth

I miss it

I miss the honesty the innocence

the wide eyed naiveté'.

We've got smart phones and I-Pads

digital cameras and computers.

But we've lost our sense of joy I think

our sense of wonder at it all.

To tell the honest truth

I miss it.

Lodestone of The Heart

No matter what I do

or what upon I try to focus

it seems as if it's all in vain.

For in the end I go back

to that place out there

out there on the prairie.

That place where I am drawn

like to a lodestone

a lodestone of the heart

People tell me I should change

put them from my mind.

Some folks say that they're too saccharin

too cloying or too sweet

these dreams I see of my plains.

And I've heard it said

the words I write are not complex enough

lack the gravitas to be taken seriously

'cause they don't lay the human psyche bare.

When all is said and done

those dreams I see of my plains

are as real to me

as that anvil sitting on that stump

sunk in the ground in the shop

I know it's only there behind my eyes

but the picture is so real

with all its' soot and grit and grime

that I can even see the rainbow

reflected in the cutting oil

puddled on the top.

Those curled shards of metal scrap

would flay my fingers to the bone

if I reached out to touch them.

I see him there at the anvil

the muscles of his arms and shoulders

beneath the fabric of his shirt

bunch and swell

seem to grow to twice their size

then slacken and relax

with the rise and fall of the hammer.

Sparks in showers

spew from measured strokes

and a sound so very like

the ringing of a distant bell.

I can taste the metal taint

of burning coal upon my tongue.

Its' sulphur undertones

deep inside my nose

like breathing in the air

during a lightning storm.

But when the forge is cool

covered with that

piece of wooden slatted binder canvas.

When the bellows fan

that sounds just like a motor car

in a nineteen thirties drama on the radio

is still.

When the only sounds

are the sparrows chirping in the cupola

and I am sitting still and silent

then.

I am a part of everything around me

the sights the sounds the smells

are steeped within my very being.

It's why the pictures of my dreams

are so real I think.

'Cause I carry them deep inside of me

from the then to the now.

So that when I resurrect the dream

I pull the essence from the then

and that place out there on the prairie

that lodestone of the heart,

that then becomes the now.

Heaven Here on Earth

I can hear the words bounce'n 'round inside my head

like if someone talks too loud

inside an empty church.

When I was eight

they told me under penalty of death

it was absolutely FORBIDDEN

to set even one bare foot

in Grandma's berry patch at the farm.

Five rods on a side

that berry patch

that sat up there up top the prairie roll

There were those

who thought it was

over-large by half

but along about

the middle of July

it could'a been twice that size

and still it wouldn't

have been too large for me

If you had a choice

you really didn't want

to be without your shoes

when you're on a mission clandestine

in Gramma's berry patch

It's because

there's something in the ashes

from the kitchen stove.

See those berries really like those ashes

So every time

my Grandpa cleans the grate

he spreads em' in the berry patch

and there's a lotta clinkers in that ash

black volcanic glass

could cut a foot to smithereens

if a person wasn't careful

And I'd be standing there

in my striped bibs

Summer sun streaming down

and 'cause we mostly went that way

in summer time

my feet were bare and ankle deep

in the dusty dry of July.

And it looks to me

cuz those berry canes

are level with my eyes

that there are berries

far as the eye can see.

And I know that it's a sin

that I'm headed straight to hell when I die

but I can't help myself

as I step gingerly

so as not to cut my feet to smithereens

into that land of forbidden fruit

into that patch of ground

where Gramma's berries are.

And those berries

are puckering my mouth with their sweetness and their tart.

Kinda like potato chips

those berries.

It's humanly impossible

to be eating only one.

Oh you may try to fool yourself

but once that burst

of bright red flavor

flows across your toungue

fills your mouth to overflowing

you will know

without a conscious thought

what I knew

at the age of eight.

If raspberry number one is really good

when you eat a couple hundred more

you won't need to worry

about the after life

cuz you will be already

in heaven here on earth.

No Big Deal

The doors and windows of the house

been covered twenty years when she called.

"It's no big deal"

she said.

"If you don't want it I'll just burn it "

she said.

That Chinese Elm

on the North side of the yard

out there at the farm.

It died you know

that Methuselah of trees.

Been there nigh on eighty years ...

"It's no big deal"

she said.

"I know you've got that fireplace"

"thought you might could use it."

"No matter though."

"it's gotta come down anyway."

"It's no big deal"

she said ....

I used to climb that old tree

scrape my forearms raw on the bark

when I was eleven or so ...

And see that patch of dirt

bare of grass between the roots?

It's where we set the circus up

when I was eight.

And ten foot out in front

the spot the wicket went for croquet.

And hanging there

eight foot off the ground

the birdhouse that my Grandpa built

in nineteen fifty seven.

"If you don't want it I'll just burn it "

she said.

"It died you know" ....

"It's no big deal"

she said .

The Weather

Perspectives of a January Night

Winter's stormy afternoon

gives way to stormy night.

Just beyond the fragile bones of the barn

waves of snow and wind

flail themselves against the walls

like a giant whale at breach.

Inside, horse manure and sweat soaked harness leather

file down the teeth of the weather

and when the great white whale of winter

sucks in her breath once more

pulls the wind past the walls

till my eardrums ache with the pressure

and the windows in the loft

are so tight agains their frames

that they no longer rattle.

The horses

noses in their mangers

ignore the storm and munch.

Autumn Air

When the sun is past midway

in it's austral journey

and it's starting to appear

a little watered to the eye.

When the temperatures at night

drop well below the freezing mark

and those damn mosquitoes

have long since given up the fight.

When I'm walking through a shelter belt

and fallen leaves

boil up around my feet

and Alice Slough is bivouac

to a hundred thousand ducks and geese.

It's then the golden days of summer

surrender to the polished amber of the fall.

It's the air I think,

mostly it's the air.

Looking at the world

through the crystal Autumn air

When it Isn't Autumn

It's that time between All Hallows and Thanksgiving

when it isn't autumn anymore.

When I can hear the whistle

of Lady Winter's train coming 'round the bend.

When it's cold enough to see your breath

but the world is mostly yet

wearing shades of brown and grey.

When the sun has lost it's punch

and the color in your cheeks isn't from the heat

rather it's the lack thereof.

When the final flocks of geese,

are gone from sight and sound

and the leaves that fell those weeks ago

no longer swirl and eddy in the wind.

It's when I walk the shelter belts

of my prairie home

and the flicker there coming through the trees

is the light of almost winter

when it isn't autumn anymore.

Morning Hasn't Hit it Yet

It's one of those days

on my Northern Plains

one of those glorious days

between the Equinox

and All Hallows

When the sun is high and bright

when a cloud or two or three

drifts slowly with the breeze

across the cobalt sky

and it's cool enough

there's still frost on the grass

where the morning hasn't hit it yet.

There's a hint of burning leaves

tickles my awareness

and in my reverie

that smell becomes an odor

sanctified somehow

like incense

in an open air cathedral.

I used to think when I was young

when I'd lie there in the prairie grass

on my back looking up

that God was closer there

underneath that sky

when the sun was high and bright

and the frost was still upon the grass

where the morning hadn't hit it yet.

Winter Dreams

It's when the blizzard rages

and the windows rattle in their frames

that I think about my winter dreams.

It's when I pull the comforter

up around my ears.

It's sitting by a fireplace

with strains of Vivaldi

imaging the wind.

It's when I breathe an opening

in the rime upon the window glass

to see how high the drifts have become.

It's when I gaze across a prairie etherized

beneath a moon as slender as a host.

When the storm has fled

and the silence has become

a thing of form and substance

that I think of things

like the memories

of my winter dreams.

Cold

Cold that has you breathing through your nose
cause if you don't you know your teeth might break.
Still silent windless cold.

Cold so quiet

you can hear the beating of your heart.

Cold so quiet

the silence seems to come in waves
that pound inside your ears.

Cold so quiet

the sound of branches
splitting on the trees
on the slide to minus forty
makes you jump almost out of your skin.

The kind of cold

that even if you think

you're not thinking about it

you're thinking about it.

Cold that IS.

From the Day of All Saints,

to that of Saint Patrick,

cold that simply

IS

It's five o-clock in the afternoon

full night in the solstice north.

His frosted breath floats skyward

as soon as it leaves his nose.

His world is of the cold.

The combers on the drifted ocean of snow

the crystal shards of ice

suspended in the air

like frozen faery dust to light his path.

He hefts his sled a fraction higher so it doesn't slip.

His Christmas sled,

the sled he keeps beside his bed

so he can touch the wood that glows like polished amber.

So he can slide his fingers along the runners

runners the color of the poinsettias

that decorate the altar at church.

So he can reach and touch it while he sleeps.

He loves the sound those runners make

sliding on the snow

defining the silence of the night.

The numbing cold that grabs his face

chills it to the bone

and the way his tears freeze in droplets to his lashes

in the downhill breeze.

He loves the stars

bright against the coal black winter sky.

He loves the solitude

the waking of the Northern Lights

like window sheers in God's own parlor

furling and unfurling in an unseen wind.

These are the times he feels his smallness

his insignificance.

These are the times

when he almost tastes the answers

to the questions at the edge of his understanding.

Lady Winter watches the boy.

Smiles to herself as he struggles to comprehend.

Knowing his words are yet too small

to attempt to define the undefinable

Except that it's cold

really cold.

Frozen Smoke

The Arctic Owl lit soundlessly

on snow like frozen smoke.

She had no care for the frigid beauty of the night

the shadows of the trees

that stretched themselves

like dappled charcoal renderings.

She lit without a sound.

A ghostly apparition

that when she took to wing once more

left a darkened stain

where once had been a rabbit

on snow like frozen smoke .

Winter Shadows

Spare and underfed
shadows are mostly
shy in winter time.
They leap out though
December afternoons
dance blue grey upon the snow
to celebrate the solstice.

Winds of Winter

Fifty rods or so west and north

of the house

a line of sixteen cottonwoods

stands perimeter.

They shed their leafy glow in winter time.

Their naked limbs

like bony fingers

clawing at the wind.

When shadows are the longest

and the sun has gone on holiday.

When the cold has become

a being sentient

and the banks of snow

that embrace the sleeping trees

are taller than my head.

It is then the winds of winter

sound through those cottonwoods

like a distant train at speed.

And there!

Beyond that sound that ears can hear

there's a feeling reaches past

that winter wind

to the underpinnings of my soul.

Dakota Spring

Floating there just above the world's edge

through veils of clouds so thin they almost aren't there

a pale disc is the sun.

The air itself seems to glow

like a million pearls lighted from within.

There's a fullness here

an earthiness you can taste.

It's a moment when the air is charged by God

with a kind of secret power

gives it weight

substance.

When

last years leaves peer out from under melting snow

When

rivulets of melt trickle to the music of the plains

flow over frozen still prairie grasses

morph quiescent coulees into raging torrents.

When

panes of ice fracture with the sound of breaking glass.

When

Lady Winter's palfrey white

is enough removed to be remembered wistfully.

Not as the rearing steed she truly was.

When

the morning frost

is a cleansing shower dripping from the trees

the Mother Prairie stirs

tastes the air

of Her Dakotah spring.

In Winter Time

Were you ever at the lake in winter time?

It makes a sound you know

when it's making ice.

A low pitched rumbling

like elephants in murmured conversation

across a frozen veldt.

Were you ever at the lake in winter time

and felt you were an interloper

interrupting something spiritual?

When the silence was so deep

your words would fall unuttered from your mouth?

Have you ever felt a storm

tear apart a winter night?

You really can't appreciate Vivaldi

till you do.

Were you ever at the lake in winter time

watched Aurora harem dance across the Northern sky?

Seen smoke blue snow beneath the solstice moon

or heard the music

of a million crystal chandeliers

when the ice piled up in spring?

Though I am alone and gone from there

I have them with me still

those feelings and those memories.

Were you ever at the lake in winter time?

Hollow of The Wind

I was casting out my net

trying to catch a thought

when it slipped into my mind

as easily, as comfortably

as remembering the color

of my daughter's eyes.

When I heard that sound

that sound the wind does make

flowing through a line of cottonwoods

in wintertime.

In wintertime

when dried out leaves

swirl in eddies

like cast off summer frocks

out of vogue.

In wintertime

when January's wind

leaps from tree to naked tree

building on the sound

that is at first beneath our notice

so much a part of what is real

has it become.

It is a sound

that has a hollowness about it

that reverberates

against the walls of itself.

Makes me want

to shed my skin

crawl inside that hollow place

feel the free.

There are those

who hear the wind

in only one dimension

poor unfortunates

their hearts are walking with a limp

unable

to step outside themselves

crawl inside that hollow place

that hollow of the wind.

Wrinkle In The Drift

Sometimes of a Sunday in the summer

we'd have a picnic at the spring.

Dad would drive with Grandpa on the passenger side

and me between them squeezed into the middle.

My little brother Darrel

rode in back with Mom and Gram

and baby Mary there in Momma's lap.

Southeast of town five six miles

down a dusty prairie path

there's a grove of trees

grows there in a rift

where the land just sort of billowed

fell into a wrinkle

a wrinkle in the Drift.

A darkling wooded glen

I used to tell myself

was a slice of Minnesota

got misplaced

got stuck out here in Dakotah

stuck out here in the drift.

Mom and Gram would fix the lunch

while we men

took the path to the spring

at the bottom of the rift

It was as if we stepped into another world

A world we knew could not exist

out here in the drift.

A world of oak and beech and cottonwood

with sunlight leaking through

in glaucous drips

And it seemed

all the more intense

the silence

with the burble gurgle of the spring

there at the bottom

the bottom of the rift

I didn't have the words

to describe the way I felt

I simply knew.

This hallowed glen.

The endless drift beyond.

Are part of me and I of them.

And in my dreams today.

I venerate my memories of that place and time.

And when my spirit thirsts

I return again to that spring

at the bottom of the rift.

In that wrinkle

that wrinkle in the drift.

Winter Trails

Winter trails fade

thaw

in the warmth of a springtime sun

Sleep

through stick horse summers

BB guns and bicycles

cops and cowboys and baseball bats.

In October they rouse.

Stretch.

Begin searching about ...

for snow.

In The Lee

They're one of natures nearly perfect things I think.

Their sculpted curves

exquisite in their symmetry

and though they only last a season

like a comet circling the sun

they come around again

when those winter storms

scream down from the North

sculpt those drifts of snow

in the lee.

Honed to an edge by the wind

like a wave breaking on a beach

it nearly curls around upon itself.

Even as a child

I saw beauty in those drifts

a surface so pristine

to mar it seemed a sacrilegious act.

A week or two into spring

that drift has nearly disappeared

nothing but a wedge of ice remains

thirty foot end to end.

It's melted girth will keep that piece of ground

green till summer wanes.

And then

a little past All Hallows Eve

like a comet circling the sun

those winter storms

scream down from the North

and sculpt a drift of snow

in the lee.

Snow-fences

That snow-fence canted forty-five degrees

where the NP rails cut the prairie roll.

You could see them all the way from town

their profile stark against the sky.

The angles and the shapes

that lent themselves to our imaginations

became a hundred different where's and when's.

A pirate ship ravaging the Spanish Main

a clipper sailing "round the horn"

or a Viking raider on a strafing run.

It was winter though when they were in their element.

When they gave birth to drifts the size of battleships.

We built entire cities in the caverns that we carved in

those drifts.

They're gone today of course

like so many things of the world I occupied.

That snow-fence out there on the prairie roll

so unimportant as to warrant not a thought

as it was swept into the bin of that that was.

Railroads to this day need to operate on level or nearly level ground. To that end about three quarter mile east of Alice is a cut through a prairie roll engineered by the old NP to do just that.. The snow fences there kept the winter snows from filling the cut and blocking the tracks. They were around 12 feet high and in winter produced a drift of snow 12 feet deep and a 1/4 mile long. a winter paradise for a bunch of prairie kids.

When It Rains

I love it when it rains

the softly muted patter

on mossy wooden shakes.

The trickle and the gush

of the downspout at the corner of the house.

I love the air freshly scrubbed and filled with wet.

The muffled rustle and the earthiness of sodden leaves

plowed through by my feet.

I love the shelter of a giant elm

when dripping drops

light on their feet as prima ballerinas

piaffe down from leaf to leaf.

I love the call of Canada geese

out of a grey and swollen sky.

And I love to share a fire with Vivaldi

when it rains

Silence

Be still...

Marvel at what peace there is in silence.

Silence

that thing beyond the sound of soughing cottonwoods

in a breeze so light I wonder if it's really there.

Silence

the way the world holds its' breath

when a blizzard flails itself to nothingness

Silence

the empty space when a meadowlark has ceased to sing.

It's that which is the other side

of the swirl and swish of grass around my knees.

Silence

the thing that separates, the thing remaining

when the last migrating goose has ceased to call.

Amidst the noise and haste

be still

marvel at what peace there is

in silence.

Fog

There's something skirts reality

in a fog.

There's something hidden there inside it's damp

that opens my awareness.

Unseen things

that often go unnoticed or unfelt

take on form and meaning.

When that opaque shroud

that makes my words fall dead

inches from my mouth

steals silently upon the scene

the world becomes enhanced somehow.

The random drip of dew

falling from the leaves

The solitary call of a bird

blinded by the mist...

and all surrounded by the quiet,

that is ...

in a fog...

October Rain

Foam flecked waves

scud across grey water

as squalls of rain lash the porch

and the smell of wet and last years leaves

soak the air.

In our cocoon of eider down

she sleeps.

Her still small face lighting up my day.

And as I lean

to kiss her cheek

the whisper of a smile

ghosts across her lips.

Sleep on

much loved daughter of mine.

Sleep on.

Her smile lingers just a moment

and another squall lashes the porch.

Rare and Wonderful

It's one of those days my Granddad used to say

one of those

rare and wonderful summer days.

When the breeze is not

a thing that's felt or heard

but a silhouette

of shifting shades and colors

in the grass.

When the blue above is unsullied

by nary a hint of white.

When the hunting call of a hawk

serves only to define the stillness.

When the hum of tires

on an asphalt motorway

is a sacrilege of the gravest order.

In those moments

I am come to something

other

other than I am

It is as if I pass

through a kind of portal

transcending time and space.

I don't think this day

is worthy of the now.

So I'll pass it through

transport it to my used to be.

where this day will never end

where this day will always be

a day forever

rare and wonderful

Dakotah Wind

She's alive you know

my Dakotah Wind

She calls to me

knows my name

I feel her speak in a hundred different tongues.

We're intimate you see

my Wind and I

I view the world through eyes not mine

look down upon my meager self

sense that there is something deeper

something spiritual

in the power of her summer storm

sense that there is something deeper

something near divine

in the elemental force of her blizzard loosed

sense that there is something more

sense that there is something

in my Wind that's Holy

We're intimate you see

my Wind and I

Fall Nineteen Eighty Nine

I really couldn't say
what brought her to my mind today
I haven't seen my friend Gertie
since the fall of nineteen-eighty- nine
saw her at the "Hunter's Supper"
at St Henry's church
I recall cause Meg was ten months old
she could walk already but wobbled when she did.
Gertie sat there in the basement
in one of those old church pews
like the rest of us
waiting for the call to supper.
When Meaghan tripped
and fell against her leg.
My friend Gertie laughed
and helped my Meaghan to her feet.
I always loved old Gertie's laugh.
Pitched up sharp and high
with a little sort of raucous note.
It always kind of reminded me
'cause of Gertie's hair

of a plump Rhode Island Red
laughing with the world.
Gertie ran the postal service
in my Dakotah town
for about a thousand years I think.
She was long retired
that fall of nineteen eighty nine
and I was over twenty years an exile
gone from home for school and livelihood.
I was one of those that periodically returned.
Like a salmon
back to the stream where they were spawned.
By summer nineteen-ninety
my friend Gertie had departed.
I was glad I'd got to see her one more time
At that "Hunter's Supper" at the church
The fall of nineteen-eighty-nine.
I really couldn't say
what brought her to my mind today
there was a time when I thought
my thoughts were dominoes
each one set on end
waiting to tap the next
and on and on and on.
But now I know that dominoes

are too much organized and boring

to reflect the way I think.

I think a little thing

and a hundred thousand thoughts are flung about.

I even get a little sad sometimes

when a thought I thought gets left behind

that I might have, should have, thought about.

But it or I too slow in getting to the station

to catch the speeding train that is my brain.

Awhile ago a far flung thought

landed on a friend of mine from years ago.

My friend and I would get together periodically

for dinner and a lively conversation.

To my Northern Plains he wasn't native

from New York State if I recall

he'd searched an almanac before he came

for information on Dakotah.

Surprised and pleased he was to find

it only snows half as much in North Dakotah

as it does where he calls home.

With that he looked me in the eye

a rather baleful stare me thought.

The Almanac didn't say, he muttered

that the snow in North Dakotah

never melts.

It's true enough I guess

That North Dakotah winters are mostly pretty cold.

In that stretch of months

from All Saints Feast to the Ides of March

it almost never gets to melting.

You've probably heard about

our fabled January thaws.

Once in awhile a very great while

it actually gets up close to freezing.

When the temp will rise to thirty degrees or so

for a day or two or maybe even three,

icicles drip from a couple of eaves

a snowman or two get built

and then it cools down

freezes up

nothing moves.

It's winter again on our northern plains

till it starts to melt for real

when the Mother Prairie looks at her watch

and finally declares, "It's spring".

So my thoughts are tearing along

in no particular direction.

When it occurs to me, that there, right there,

Right there where we're sitting he and I,

there was a mile of ice above our heads

ten thousand years ago.

Spring was slow in coming in the ice age too.

When that glacier finally thawed

it left behind a bunch of potholes we call sloughs.

So maybe you ask yourself

who gives a rusty rip?

About cold and glaciers and sloughs and stuff?

Well, it's actually quite simple

in a complicated way.

Cause my Dakotah prairie

and it's million pothole sloughs,

is a North American nursery.

Cause all those sloughs

are full to overflowing in the spring

on account of the snow waits till then to melt.

So when the Mom and Daddy ducks fly north

they don't see a bunch of sloughs down there

they see ready made mallard mansions

big old duck developments,

condo's for canard's.

So you probably ask yourself

who gives a rusty rip?

So I guess I'll have to explain it to you.

When all those baby ducks get raised

get to be full grown

our North Dakotah sloughs

become a hunters paradise.

The deal is this you see

if it hadn't have been for that glacier

ten thousand years ago

and a million prairie sloughs

that are houses for a zillion ducks

that brought the hunters here

there never ever would have been

a "Hunter's Supper" at St. Henry's.

And I'd a' never been home

to say goodbye to Gertie

in the fall of nineteen-eighty-nine.

The Land

Not With My Eyes

I have a photo that I took

forty years or so ago.

Nothing very special actually

Truth be told

there really wasn't much to see

with my eyes.

Just my rolling northern steppe

grass up past my knees

and not a tree in sight.

But when I looked close

I could see

a remnant overgrown

of a prairie road

that veered off to the right

disappeared

between the grassy rolls.

A subtle thing

in shades of green on green

almost invisible

whispers of a world thats lost.

And I guess that it's imagination

or something very like it

'Cause when I look

I swear that time wraps around itself

and I see

the world that's down that prairie road

disappeared between the grassy rolls

not with my eyes.

Island in The Drift

It's called "The Drift"

that east Dakotah plain

and there's a piece of ground

fifteen miles from my town

like an island there

an island in the Drift.

A patch of ancient wildness

thirty miles or so across.

A place I go

when I want to lose the world

leave behind the lane that's fast

trade it for the one that's vast.

A hundred centuries barely changed

this gravel island in the Drift.

Dropped here by that hunk of ice

ten thousand years ago.

It isn't much worth a damn

for growing things

'Cause if you take away the grass

that sand just starts to blow.

It's ageless beauty has no need

for the trappings of today

It's maybe partly why I love it so.

There is a nearly undefinable

hauteur

about this place.

It seems almost to be

self aware

Makes me want to spread my arms

wrap it up in my embrace.

The grassy, sandy, rolling drift

The wooded river bottom

brush and trees so thick

I have to leave my horse

go afoot.

There's a silence here

so deep

that I can feel it's hum

inside the bones of my skull.

Where a Prairie Chicken

booming out his love

or cicada sawing down the day

only paints the picture brighter.

I find it easy to confuse today

confuse reality and myth.

And the longer I'm away

the more convinced am I

That my reality is an island there

an island in the Drift.

For The Lack of Them

When I turn my thoughts to the past

think back upon my years

it's plain the world of my youth climbed inside of me

resides here still within my soul.

One can't help but notice

sounds out here on the prairie

because there's mostly such a lack of them

Like the breeze borne whisper of the grass

cottonwoods like morning tides over shallow shoals

in the paleness of the dawn.

And still

I feel the stillness beat a cadence in my ears

when a blizzard blows itself to nothingness

or that serenity

that is somehow totally defined

by a single Meadowlark at song.

It resides here still

that world of my youth

resides here still within my soul.

Greasy Grass Country

In the tongue of the Dakotah

it is the country of the grass.

The grass thats greasy in the wind

For the way it slips and swirls

whispers in the breeze

catches light like waves

in a sea of opalescent green

It isn't just the wind

there's a feeling too thats there

of a majesty beneath the sound

that slips within my soul.

I ask myself sometimes

is it an echo

of when the world came first to be?

A kind of grace note maybe?

On an instrument played by God

when she holds her finger on the key

plays a note so low it almost isn't there.

I wonder too if others hear it

or is it only me?

I wish that I

could climb inside that note somehow

feel the world from there.

It is the elemental essence that I feel I think.

A reminder

that spirit never sleeps

In the country of the grass

that's greasy in the wind

Great Grass Sea

There's a piece of ground south of town

just north of Alice Slough

A primal atoll in the Great Grass Sea

A native patch of waist high brome

I don't think was ever broke.

Used to be a soddy there a hundred years and more ago.

And when the sun is nearly set

you can see the shadow still

that snakes along the prairie roll

of the two track from the century past.

These days a cottonwood

eighty foot if it's an inch

grows between those tracks

so long it's been since they were driven on.

On the northern shore of Alice Slough

the land rolls up in a wrinkle

to a bluff thats likely sixty foot.

Old timers say a jump was there years and years ago.

I always knew it was a special place.

When the wind flows down to the North
careening off that bluff
it billows and swirls the waist high brome
playing the light like mother of pearl
in a silhouette of itself.

There's a piece of ground south of town
just north of Alice Slough
a primal atoll in the Great Grass Sea
If you lie on your back in the waist high brome
thats not the wind flowing down to the North
it's the whispering sigh of the prairie
telling the secrets of the Great Grass Sea

Out The Back Door

Out the back door to the East

a couple hundred feet away

a little house and weathered barn

sit on a city block

encircled by a rusted barb wire fence

that leans and sways

like a hired hand on Saturday night.

There are trees that grow

along that barb-wire line.

Box-elder trees and ash

twenty thirty foot in height

three four dozen cottonwoods

even an errant silver maple

that found its way out here from Minnesota.

Those trees are intertwined

along that line of fence

like the chorus line at Rockefeller Centre.

The wind it eddies there

past that line of trees

and in the middle of the block

the grass it shifts and ripples

catches rays of light in a hundred shades of green

like the writhing spine of some imaginary serpent

beneath the waves on this prairie sea.

When I was young

I'd dive beneath those waves

and listen to my world.

I'd listen to the murmur of the trees

the quiet hiss of the wind

as it swirled through that patch of grass

encircled by a rusted barb wire fence

out the back door to the East.

Tundra Bound

I feel a stirring deep within

before I'm even conscious of their calls.

As I gaze upon their chevrons winging north

tears start welling in my eyes

There is a link that's forged

'tween they and I

outside the real

For in that moment

that solitary moment

suspended there in time

the world does not exist

save for me

and those Canadiens

tundra bound.

Song of the Lark

I feel as though I'm swimming

in a green and glaucous sea

As a wind thats nearly nonexistent

swirls the grass around my knees

The crystal shard of a Lark in song,

slices through the almost silence,

of a sky so wide I nearly have to catch my breath.

And if I could

somehow see her song

that song would be a cataract of light

in my private dark

Am I being selfish?

Sharing not this moment locked in time?

We're the only ones alive you see,

my meadowlark and I

and I know that she is singing

just for me

Sea of Grass

I am the sea of grass
roiling in the wind.

I am Cottonwoods
along prairie streams.

I am the Canada Goose
winging my way to summer.

I am Redwings
bobbing on cattails

I am Willows
in grassy ravines

I am the Meadowlark
singing in the silence.

I am the Coyote waiting.

I am the Prairie Dog watching.

I am the Redtail Hawk
riding the thermals in a blue enamel sky.

I am the Buffalo Common
vast
timeless

I hear the ghosts
of a hundred million bison
whispering.

I shed tears with Crazy Horse and Sitting Bull.

I held the children of the Grapes of Wrath
to my ancient bosom.
Their abandoned homesteads
bleaching in the sun
like skeletons of broken dreams.

I am the plains.

My ancient trails trod by numbers uncounted

obscured by the dust of time.

I am the Great Drift Prairie.

My primal pastures

gone to cattle herds and wheat fields

and ranches and farms and towns

and pickup trucks and diesel fumes

and grain dust and cattle dung.

Elevators and oil derricks

silhouette my prairie sunset.

But if you look past the trappings of today

there are times even now

when the light is right

you can see them still

the ghost herd

plying the waves

on my Sea of Grass.

No One Much Remembers

I came across a line the other day
sort of gave me pause.
" A walk among the tombstones "
was what it said.
I got to thinking about that line
the many meanings it could have for me.
Like those graves out there
on the bluff by Alice Slough.
Where a century past and more
where that family was lost.
You can see the shimmer still
in the grass
of that special shade of green
when the light is angled right
on those graves.
But no one much remembers anymore
those markers made of cottonwood.
No one much remembers anymore.

A couple miles east of here

in the valley of the Maple River

just upstream from Uncle Ernie's Garden.

Those teepee rings that I found

when I was nine.

I felt the spirits in those stones

of those people that are no longer here.

Heard their thoughts whispering to me.

It went to hay-land though

that patch of ground,

sometime in the sixties.

And no one much remembers anymore

those teepee people and their ways.

No one much remembers anymore.

Not so long ago I penned a line or two

about an old abandoned farm,

where I used to play when I was ten.

How the timbers of that barn

were the bony ribs of a prairie dinosaur

gone extinct.

About the rope marks on the elm tree branch

where the children's swing used to hang.
But no one much remembers anymore.
Of the farm, nothing left to speak of
except a little hiccough in the prairie roll
that no one much remembers anymore.

The places that I walked
mostly hollow now
vacant shells of the then.
Nothing left to touch
but the tombstones
that no one much remembers anymore.

Still Learning

I've seen waist high grass

mime the prairie wind.

Surfed the shoals

of a sea of cottonwoods.

I've watched a fog

belly crawl ravines

in early spring

climbed inside a winter solstice

and paced the length

of December shadows on the snow.

I've felt the silence

penetrate the ashes of my bones.

Seen Aurora's veil ripple in the polar breeze.

I've heard blizzard driven winds

blow like whales at breach

and wept real tears

at vacant farms and empty towns

that felt like cinders of burnt out suns.

I've spoken to the ghosts

that wander here

listened to their songs.

For I know the day will come

when I will join them.

This day though

I wander still.

Still learning the words that I will sing

when I am summoned home.

The Crucible

You ask me why

why do I go back?

I go back to experience once again

that feeling that I left

back there on the prairies of my youth.

I go back to trees

that whisper in the wind.

To the sound of rain

in a prairie thunderstorm.

I go back to summer days of china blue

and to autumn's amber glow.

I go back to tumbleweeds,

and bleak and brown Novembers.

To a sea of grass

imaging the wind.

I go back to watermelon sunsets

painted on a sky so wide,

they alone

confirm the existence of God.

I go back

to realize the moments that define me.

To experience the crucible that forged me.

I go back to the openness

to fill my emptiness.

Alice Slough

Alice Slough is two miles south of my home town give or take. A mile long or so and half that wide about. Shaped sort of like a pear with the fat end on the west. It angles to the north a little in the east the narrow end cocked up a bit. Ten foot deep in years that are wet it's a bowl of alkali with a brackish puddle in the middle in the dry. Clouds of dust swirl in the wind like an other worldly landscape in a painting done by Dali. A bluff thats likely sixty foot is the shoreline on the north and for eighty years it was the area garbage dump. People pulled their trucks or wagons to the edge and tossed whatever they were tossing off the bluff. Every now and again a crawler tractor would push the garbage farther out, push it off the bluff. I hunted rats out there when I was young till I heard one time that if you should see a rat there's a hundred others that you don't. Gave me the creeps for sure and I quit right then hunting rats. They closed down that old dump in nineteen seventy four or five and most everything got buried. There's two, three, cottonwoods growing now likely thirty feet where the P.V. Grain and Feed used to dump their tailings.(That place always was the best for hunting rats) I wish sometimes I had a drill like the ones that scientists use to core the ice in Greenland. I'd drill down in that old dump find all sorts of things. I'd find buffalo bones more than likely and arrowheads and such at the bottom. When I was ten or so old Charlie Multz told me the bluff was a buffalo jump a zillion years or so ago.

Alice Slough is a secret place of mine. I suppose it's hard to think of a place that size as secret. It's really just my secret privately I guess. I'd haul garbage to that old dump when I was a lad I'd be three hours gone. I'd sit out there in that marsh Redwings all around bobbing on their cattails singing just for me. I'd sit so still they'd come right to me so close that I could reach right out and touch them. If I hold my head just right I can hear those Redwings yet today as clearly as they were more than half a century past

There's about a million ducks in Alice Slough, Mallards, Teal, Redheads, and about a dozen others. There's Mud hens too, some people call them Coots but Grandpa called them Mud Hens and that was good enough for me. Ducks and geese are good to eat but Mud hens? My Grandpa told me, "if you put a Mud hen in a pot and stew it for a week then throw away the bones and meat you could probably use the broth for killing weeds." And then there are the Geese. I love the Geese. Brilliant Snows big buff and black Canadiens but my favorites are the Swans. My lovely incredible swans. "A thing of beauty is a joy forever " wrote Keats and as far as I'm concerned he was writing about those swans. I can't not feel a stirring deep inside an almost reverence at their presence. When swans come swimming by crowds of geese and ducks move aside to let them pass. Like Greta Garbo walking down a crowded street swans just seem indifferent to their own magnificence. I'd lay for hours watching them. I'd try to climb behind their eyes try to see the world the way they do.

You can always know hunters from out of state. They're the ones in camouflage. A thousand shotgun shells hanging from their custom made hunting vests. They're the ones with brand new trucks with foreign plates, boots from L.L.Bean that lace up to the knee. They're the ones with shotguns with inlaid silver filigree. They're the ones that look like pictures from a magazine and are dumb as a box of rocks mostly.

Sixteen years I was, that fall of nineteen sixty three. The truck was shiny new, a nineteen sixty four "Power Wagon" one of those fancy four wheel drives with great big tires jacked way up so you couldn't see inside the box. Foreign plates, Minneapolis. "Just put the bag in the corner of the box " My Daddy said of the groceries I was carrying. I had to climb the hitch to get up high enough. There were no ducks in that box no Mallards no Teal. There were no geese no Snows no Canadiens. The five Swans were something Truman Capote could write about, bright red blood splashed against the white. Jet black beaks agape, tongues forever silenced. Slender three foot necks stretched out parallel. A bloody white musical staff on which the fates had penned a requiem from Tchaikovsky.

I heard a rancher in Sentinel Butte, bought the guns and truck from Game and Fish. "You can't put a price on loveliness" so the saying goes. But those swans cost those guys two thousand bucks a bird in fines.

You can't mistake a swan for a goose if you're smarter than a box of rocks.

From the wagon road in nineteen hundred and five to highway thirty eight today. The picture of Alice Slough looks pretty much the same. It's a game preserve these days an honest to goodness"Waterfowl Production Area". And this past summer the first in over forty years two pair of swans nested and raised their broods. And I never really realized how much that they were missed till they came back and a piece of life that had been absent returned to what it used to be at Alice Slough.

The Hartle Place

A skirmish line of cottonwoods
twenty rods end to end
along what used to be a fence line
is all thats left
of the Hartle place.

If you look close
you can see
a darker shade of green
where the wheat field grows
where the barn and pasture used to be.

Even yet today
when they're working up the ground
where sat the house and yard
with its lilac bushes and caragana hedge.
Like accidental archaeologists
a rusted tin
a shard of glass

memories of a century past

are brought to light.

But a skirmish line of cottonwoods

twenty rods end to end

next to a patch of green

and a hundred years of memories

are all thats really left

of the Hartle place.

A Hundred Yards Down From The Notch

Do you remember those graves I talked about out by Alice Slough? Last time I looked for them the markers were completely gone. Hand carved cottonwood they'd been. Way too gnarly for building with but farmers like it for wagon beds and such. And markers of course. Markers for a grave when there isn't any stone to be had. Doesn't matter though even cottonwood won't last through a century of weather on the plains of North Dakotah.

Up close you can't see them, the graves. They're on that prairie roll a hundred yards down from the notch. Up close you can't see them. You have to get back. Back across the neck of Alice Slough. And even then you only see them in the summertime, when the grass is way above your knees. And even then, even then you have to wait. Wait until the afternoon when the sun is coming from the side. When it hits the prairie grass at that sideways angle and that tiny difference in the shade of green shows up. And the lines that shimmer in the grass across the neck of Alice Slough outline and become the graves. Most folks think the notch is a gravel pit. Left here by that glacier ten thousand years ago. But the one that you and I are looking at? The one looks over Alice Slough? It's all that's left, left of the house that Sophie built a hundred and forty years ago, a dugout on the prairie roll.

Seven months along our Sophie was when she and Joseph left their home. Left Bohemia behind. They were of the first, first of the immigrants, to listen to the dream. Leave all they knew, trade it for a place in the wilds of Dakotah.

Maybe they shouldn't have made the trip. Maybe they should have stayed there in New York. Or even in St. Paul. And that wagon trip from where the rail line quit, out here to the plains, maybe it was too rough. Sophie doesn't question. Question the will of God. She stops for just a moment now and again. When a special kind of light falls on the grave of baby Ida Marie. A hundred yards down from the notch.

They went through the motions that summer and fall Joseph and Sophia. Went through the motions of living. They finished the barn for the horses and cow. Finished the dugout on the prairie roll. And through that fall that terrible fall they mourned sweet Ida Marie.

Joseph left at dawn that day twenty December for the twenty mile ride to Fort Ransom and back. Left to buy presents and supplies for the Christmas holiday.

"Alberta Clipper" is what they're called. Those fast moving storms, Canadian born. Snow so thick you can't see your hand at the end of your arm when the temperatures drop fifty degrees in an hour and the blizzard wind tears away your very breath. She found him there that

Christmas day. Forever sleeping in the snow. Kept him in the barn until the ground thawed out enough to dig a second grave in that special light, a hundred yards down from the notch. She kept to herself after that pretty much. Not hard to do where people are scarce. I'd hear stories when I was young. How from that road, that wagon road, that skirts the edge of Alice slough. You'd sometimes see her there, tending flowers by the graves, of Joe and Ida Marie.

I wish that I had known Sophia. Sometimes I almost feel I do. Sometimes in the summer, when the grass is three foot high and I'm on that wagon road that yet today skirts Alice Slough. When sun is coming in sideways kinda. When it hits the grass at that sideways angle and that shade of green shows up across the neck of Alice Slough. I sometimes think that I can see her standing by the graves.

Standing in that special light.

A hundred yards down from the notch.

Cattails in the Fall

It was a grey-brown smell

took me there.

Took me to my Northern Plains,

in the fall.

It's when the water isn't froze just yet in the sloughs

but it's cold enough to kill you dead

if you fall in.

I can smell the grey-brown smell of cattail stems

almost froze.

Hear them riffle

like the pages of a notebook in the breeze.

There's a flock of snows on the water there

a hundred yards away.

Ghostly phantoms

fading in and out through the mist.

And of a sudden

as one

they dance across the frigid fen

take to wing.

I can smell the grey-brown smell of cattail stems

almost froze

hear them riffle in the breeze.

Back there on my Northern Plains,

in the fall.

Not a Shot Was Fired

When I make that turn

off the asphalt motorway

on to that country road

head out across the drift

though I know that it's been sixty years

am I the only one

that feels a sense of loss

a sense of being violated?

Where a pasture and a barn

a house where people lived

with lilacs and a garden

that lived and breathed where I stand

fields of beans and corn

stretch far as the eye can see today.

Where the gravel road I used to take

slowly fades and disappears

reverting to the prairie path

from whence it came.

And that patch of ground

that held a tended grove of trees

lies naked in the sun.

I feel as if I'm in

a post apocalyptic age.

Where my war was lost

and my world is a little poorer

and not a shot was fired.

A Summer Morning

Might'a been the angle of the sun that triggered me

or some such reflex thing.

'Cause suddenly

I could see the kitchen of a morning in the summertime

feel the coolness

before the cookstove fires heated up the day.

The windows were all open

and the sun of 5AM streaming through the screens

gave a golden almost luminescent hue

to the air.

Through those open panes

I could hear the bumblebees

shouldering their way through the pansies and petunias

in the box out on the sill.

I could see and feel a hundred things of that then.

The damp from where the drain

ran down the pea rock underneath the porch.

The standing stale water

where the icebox dripped into the pan.

The hint of smoke from the still cold stove

and the lingering of yesterdays loaves of bread.

I could hear my Grandma

work the handle on the pump.

That burnt red cast iron pump

it's handle worn all shiny

from sixty years of use

squeaking like a rusty gate.

And the leather washers down inside

sounding like a goose

getting strangled at the bottom of a well.

She'd put the white enamel pot on the burner top

strike a Diamond Match

and the air would smell of sulphur

as half a dozen pages of Dakotah Farmer

lit the kindling in the fire box

and the heating stove

slowly overtook the coolness

of the summer morning.

Out Here

The antimacassar she crocheted those sixty years ago

is tied up still to the faded pillow where he used to rest his head.

The jacket that he wore for chores

hangs there from its' designated nail

stitched and patched and looking like a pile of rags

she doesn't have the heart to throw it out.

His overshoes

the hightop buckle ones he wore for working in the barn

lay in the corner where he kicked them last.

And yesterday for the first time ever since he left

for only just a moment she sat down in the rocker where he used to sit

pressed her face against the old chenille spread

that covers the upholstery

smelled the smell of pipe and after shave

and that hard to put your finger on "old man smell"

she'd grown so used to over time.

And when she takes the two-wheel out for wood

she lingers there in the lean

where wood chips underfoot pad her every step

and the balsam smell that fills the air

carries with the memories of a million other thens.

Her daughters and their families

say "come on Gramma move to town

you can't stay out here by yourself."

"I know they only want what's best for me" she thinks.

"I wonder how to tell them I'm just fine."

"I'm just not ready yet for moving off the farm."

"I can't be leaving when it still,

smells like him,

out here."

Dusk

Day falls silently

into evening's waiting arms.

As crows drag darkness into being

the Mother Prairie yawns,

stretches herself

the gentle breeze of twilight

her drowsy breath of repose.

Prairie Perspective

Introduced to the Wheat field,

The Mother Prairie

felt a nameless dread.

She reflected a moment...

and thought...

Interloper!!

Uncle Ernie's Maple Valley Gardens

There used to be a place

in County Cass of North Dakotah

South of Alice, North of the Ransom County line.

You traveled down a one lane gravel road

fields and prairies on either side

and of a sudden you realize

those bushes there ahead on either side

aren't really bushes after all

they're the tops of trees

in the valley of the knee deep Maple.

The road gets narrow at valley bottom

a tiny single lane.

If you cross the Maple River

on that wooden one lane bridge

you can feel the sway and squeal

of every timber and spar

and the surface planks go ker-flump

every time a car goes over

It feels like a ride at Disneyland

a heckuva thrill when I was ten.

Still and all I was glad for solid ground just the same.

A hundred feet this side

there's a two track prairie road into the trees

sorta hard to see

from the King weeds and the Fire-bush

trying to block the view.

Ernie says having the driveway hard to find

might keep people away

that you'd just as soon not see.

Fifty yards further on

that road goes into the trees into the shadows there

a tad bit gloomy for a kid of ten fresh come from the prairie.

I was used to the sun without much shade

and this felt kinda

like entering a church that wasn't mine.

I figured God was in there too

but he might be wondering just a little about me.

In spite of it's seeming indifference to humans

I always felt included in the Mother Prairie's creation

I'd always thought I had a special place

in the universe of the plains.

Cause God could see me there in the light of the sun

I wasn't so sure about the shade.

We went through those trees

to another then

skirting the knee deep Maple.

The light ahead was like the end of a tunnel through the Hindu Kush.

We burst from the gloom in a different world

A northern plains Shangri-La.

Over sixty years and I marvel still

at the texture of that light

where the air itself seemed to glow

with a million colors we couldn't even name.

It was the Garden.

My Uncle Ernie's Maple Valley Garden.

Acres and acres of berries

and trees laden with apples

and vegetables and flowers of a hundred different kinds.

Butterflies and Dragonflies

like so many faerys flickering

on golden shafts of light.

And quiet.

Quiet so quiet I can hear the hum of a million bees

or the purring of the cat

rubbing against my cousin's leg.

There's a cabin at the garden

where cousin Ann and I would play

Prairie Soddy one day.

The Palace of Versailles the next.

The knee deep Maple, Cleopatra's Nile, Huck Finn's Mississippi

or just a place to get cool

on a July afternoon.

My cousin Ann was born in February

me the following December

Ann would say for two months we're the same'

but after February she's the oldest.

I sorta knew she just liked being boss mostly.

One day Ann wanted to be Stanley hunting Livingston

up the reaches of the Nile.

I figured she just wanted to say'Doctor Livingston I presume'

While I stood around looking dumb.

So I talked her into Lewis and Clark up the Missouri.

She was OK with that, as long as she was Lewis.

(I figured she wanted top billing)

She might want to be Sacajawea I said

being a girl and all.

Cousin Ann didn't speak

she just looked at me

like a fox would watch a rabbit.

I forgot about Sacajawea.

Thus was born the expedition of

Nineteen fifty seven

Captain Lewis declaring

'these intrepid adventurers would explore

the farthest reaches of wilderness

and reach the Pacific Ocean.'

While Captain Clarke allowed

'thats all well and good

but we have to be back by suppertime.'

About a mile up the knee deep Maple

is where we found them

In an open meadow where the grass was arm pit high

It's where we found those circles hidden there

the teepee rings from a century past.

I know that it's a little strange

but I could feel the people in those stones

hear their voices.

They spoke to me in a language

just beyond the limit of my understanding

It's been my secret all these many years

that when I touched those stones

I began to cry.

A sadness and a sense of loss

I didn't understand.

Sometimes today

I think of those stones and gone people

and I'm saddened by how little the world has changed

We still don't glory in our diversity

we decry our differences instead

and in our arrogance

try to turn others into us.

There was no radio at the garden

neither was there television.

The refrigerator was a galvanized pail on the end of a rope

fifteen foot underground.

We had a deck of cards and a checker board

a gasoline burning mantle lamp

and we were never bored.

There's great freedom in being a kid

I didn't have to feel embarrassed

at finding beauty in my world.

It wasn't about fantasy and Lewis and Clarke

it was about imagination.

It was about living

and not apologizing for being.

About being at my Uncles

Maple Valley Gardens

at the age of ten.

And pretty much knowing

that all I really needed to know about the world

was right there ...mostly.

When I was back to Alice recently I made it a point to drive out to Ernie's Maple Valley Garden just to take a stroll down memory lane. Ernie's heirs had long since sold the property and while it hadn't been used commercially the site had been left intact. The last time I'd been to the site had been over thirty years prior when I and my wife had gathered deadfall apples and taken them home and made two dozen pies, a truly lovely memory. This trip not so much, I actually drove by the site three times before I finally realized where I was. Where had been an utterly charming spot along the Maple River, with hundreds, if not thousands of wild trees, with open meadows, and a lovely Apple orchard, now looks like a bombed out area in Dresden or Berlin. Cabin gone and not a tree remains, nothing of the orchard survives, just bare ground with a few weeds growing. Sad.

I Think That I Hear God Whispering to Me

The sky is overflowing blue
on my Dakotah steppe.

Where...

Are sounds
that are the quietest
on earth.
Sounds
that seem somehow
to paint the silence on
with a brush.

Where:

breezes hum
through fences
tightly strung.

Where:

grasses to my waist
telegraph the wind.

Where:

green and silver cottonwoods
breathe the air of summer.
And a Meadowlark
sings it's notes of
solitude.

Where.

Power lines in the wind
like lyre strings
overlarge.
Vibrate
at a level
I almost only
feel.

Where.

When thunder ceases

and rain

is dripping from the leaves.

It carves

a quiet so profound

I think that I hear God

whispering to me

Grass Up to My Waist

When ever first I saw

those hay bales in the round

the snow that fell the night before looked like icing

on six foot cinnamon buns.

It was in the meadow that I saw them

that meadow in the bottom land

along the knee deep Maple

where those teepee rings

and grass up to my waist used to be.

When last I walked that native ground

the cottonwood still stood

there up top the prairie roll.

It's silhouette against the sky

a salient icon in those times.

It's all cascading thoughts anymore

of memories colliding with reality

Like hay bales in the round

where teepee rings

and grass up to my waist used to be.

Hand in Hand With God

I see why they picked this spot
those people in that other then.
It's one of those places on the plains
where it feels as if I'm standing
hand in hand with God.

Some folks think
the land's too wide somehow
the sky too overlarge
They have to take it
in smaller bites.
It's just too big
to swallow all at once.

The house still stands there in the draw
half way up that prairie roll.
The window bay still juts
where the parlor used to be
and vacant panes still stare

at the line between the earth and sky

Feral trees and bushes

ring the house today

and I will swear that I can taste

the grass that's blown and lodged

and overgrown.

I think sometimes

my Prairie Wind

let's me step outside the now

she slows the world

so I can watch

the arpeggio she plays

hear her subtle whisper in the grass

as she climbs the prairie roll

yes I see why they picked this spot

those people in that other then

it feels as if I'm standing

hand in hand with God.

Behind Our Eyes

Squadrons of Canadians

rise through morning mists.

Flying Fortresses

bent upon the millet field two miles away.

Listen!

Hear the air

rushing by their wings.

Hear their voices

as they pass the cattail copse in which I lie.

So Close.

Any closer

I could reach my hand.

Touch them.

I feel a kinship with these birds

I really can't explain.

There is another where and when

I think.

Not of this reality.

Where we're brothers

they and I

behind our eyes.

Poultice for My Soul

There's a place in North Dakota

fifteen miles or so from my town.

A place that's out of sync with time and space.

And once in every little while

when my psyche's bruised,

when the world conspires

to loose me from my sanity,

I take a trip out there

to get a poultice for my soul.

I've seen yellowed photographs

of that patch of ground.

Pictures from a hundred years and more ago.

Aside from asphalt on the surface

of the single highway going through

the land looks pretty much the same today.

My Sandhills are an ancient river delta

thirty, forty miles on a side

dropped there on the prairie by an ice age freshet

when that glacier thawed ten thousand years ago.

To follow down a township line

head into those hills

like riding on a calendar going backward

time flows in reverse

and in a mile, maybe two

a century or more will fall away

take me to a place

before the roads were there

take me to a place

there is no sound of power lines

singing in the prairie wind

take me to a place

where the high pitched whine that tires make

speeding down a motorway

hasn't been imagined yet.

And when I walk along a sandy glen or ravine

prairie grass whispering

in the almost silence

I can see the Killdeer with her imitation broken wing

running up ahead of me

see her young ones squatting on the ground

hiding in plain sight

I can hear the Coyote sneeze to clear his nose

as he passes by twenty feet away.

I can smell the dill growing wild in that place

and hear the Meadowlark

sing like she and I are all alone in the world.

Just a tattered remnant now those hills

of a Tall Grass Prairie stretched a thousand miles or more.

Kept around I think

so folks like me

with half their hearts buried in the Prairie Sod

can find a poultice for their soul.

Where Once There Was a Bridge

It's been some years

since last I visited.

Since last I traveled

this isolated stretch.

And as I top the prairie roll

begin descent into the valley just beyond.

There's nothing left this day

but the weathered concrete piers

where once there was a bridge

across the knee deep Maple.

It was unsafe they said

that wooden bridge

of eighty years.

And what was left

of it's timbers and it's spars

was disassembled

hauled away.

And there's nothing left this day

but the weathered concrete piers

where once there was a bridge

across the knee deep Maple.

The sounds of that old bridge

the buck and thump

of four by ten inch wooden planks

as vehicles passed over

recede into an ever distant past.

I still hear them though

feel that nearly visceral vibration.

And there's nothing left this day

but the weathered concrete piers

where once there was a bridge

across the knee deep Maple.

We used to fish off that bridge

my Grandad and myself.

We'd go fishing river perch

somedays even we'd catch a few.

And thirty rods or so below

There's the spot where we would skate

my brother and my Dad and I

in winter time at thirty five below.

It's been some years

since last I visited

And I have to say

I feel my pulse rate

falter just a little

when I see

there's nothing left this day

but the weathered concrete piers

where once there was a bridge

across the knee deep Maple

The Blasel Place

The house was gone forty years

when I got there to the Blasel place.

Burned to the ground they said

that Christmas Eve nineteen-hundred-fifteen

I could see the spot

whereon the house had stood

from the piers of rock

where the corners rested then

What used to be a Caragana hedge

had grown so high

it was fifteen foot, top to bottom if an inch.

Tattered lilacs stood the watch

over a pile of rubble

that had been the entrance way those years before.

I was nine years old in that then

watching my barefoot step

minding the broken glass and rusty nails in the prairie grass.

An apple tree clung to life where used to be the yard

a world of knee high grass and broken limbs and windfalls
the deer had yet to find.

Across the yard fifteen rods away
the bleached out timbers of the barn
like the ribcage of a dinosaur
through which the prairie wind
prowled and moaned.

The grove out north was sparse of trees,
from years of grazing thin.
It's the memories though
that were etched into this place
where a ten foot drift of snow
was San Juan Hill
for another nine year old
a half a century past.

You could see the marks on the cross ways branch
of the elm tree there that shaded still the yard
where a children's swing once hung
where girls in petticoats and pinafores
and boys in bibs and brogans squealed and played.

It's razed and gone today

the Blasel place.

The field whereon it sat

a minor inlet on the wide wheat sea

I'm glad that I was there

that half a century past

to save the image in my heart

of that other then

Though it's gone today from the here and now

it can't be truly lost

if it can be touched

by a memory

Beneath the Streets of Rome

I imagined then

beneath a newer sun

that I was Dakotah Sioux

hunting on the Game Trail path

there beside the knee deep Maple

It's mostly faded now that ancient track

but there are places still

where its' skeleton remains

Where echo's of

a hundred million hooves

that carved away the prairie sod

to dusty trenches three foot deep

reverberate through time

like those sacred relics beneath the streets of Rome

I see those bones tightly held

in catacombs alluvial

where bison trod those centuries ago

Though I'm just pretend Dakotah Sioux

there are places here

beside this knee deep Maple

still visible through the verdigris of time

like the sacred places

beneath the streets of Rome

The Empty There

I doubt I could recall a time I didn't notice it

that country school down the drive that angles off the section line

I doubt that I could count the times that I've passed by

seen the sun in afternoon

beat the windows into plates of burnished brass

Make it seem as if it were alive again

lighted from within

Built in nineteen hundred ten it was

three decades and a half

before ever I took breath.

By the time that I was in grade three

they closed it down

that country school.

It feels it's been a thousand years

the swings and slides and tilt around

rusted in the empty there.

I always feel

the empty there.

If I press my nose against the window pane

peer beyond the grit and grime of time

peer beyond the wood perfume of pencil sharpenings

the dried up dust of pounded out erasers

and the rows of hooks

where coats and caps and scarves once hung.

I sometimes think

that I can hear the sounds of children's voices

echo faintly through the empty there.

Been near a lifetime now

since last the school bell rang.

Almost I feel as if I hear its' sound

like someone rings it

in the empty there.

I always feel

the empty there

Symphony

Sometimes,

when I'm lying in the prairie grass

staring at the blue

I wonder at the silence

that seeps inside of me

penetrates my bones.

I wonder at the words I need

to describe infinity

or how to hear the symphony

hidden in the whisper of eternity

Old Friends Reminisce

The cottonwood had quite forgotten

the buffalo

Then the crow

mentioned the bones

bleaching in the creek bed

Honesty of Emptiness

I've heard it said

the laws of physics don't apply

out here.

Out here in my openness

Time just seems to flow

forth and back

Past and present

are the same

It is an icon

that openness

Broaching not

a compromise with sentiment

This ocean

filled with emptiness

is a seed

A seed that grows

into a million possibilities

It can be a dangerous place

to the uninitiated

But something happens here

The openness

The barrenness

The honesty and beauty

of the emptiness

are a poultice to my soul

They draw the poison out.

I Am Better For It

Almost sometimes it seems to be aware

Almost sometimes it seems to know that I am there.

Almost sometimes I feel a kind of pulse

out there

Like an unseen heart

secreted behind

the breathing of the wind

I think sometimes I hear a chant

a choir I can never see

beneath the things I see and hear

beneath the melody

the rhythm of the normal

I look beyond the sparse and spare

that is the seen

Beyond the too large sky

and horizons

way too wide

Instead of fighting and denying

the fearsome size

that seems to smite my puny human senses

with it's bored indifference to my presence.

I embrace my prairie world

let it flow

seep inside my paltry self

and I am better for it.

About October

There's something rare about October

with its honey colored air.

It doesn't seem to need the sun

it kind of glows inside itself

like looking at the world through polished amber.

There's something rare about October.

Coolness that defines its' texture on my skin.

Ripened heads of thigh high brome

that silhouette the prairie wind

and the aromatic tang of wood smoke

from an open fire.

There's something rare about October

yellowed paper cornstalks

rustling in the breeze.

The earthy smell of furrows freshly turned.

The roiling surf of cottonwoods

swaying in the wind.

The haunting call

of southward bound Canada Geese.

Dad and I tramped these plains
prairie grass tugging at our knees.
We thought that we were only walking our Dakotah home
but looking back upon those times
I think that we were actually
learning how to Be.

There's something rare about October.

Silent Stones

In a corner lonely

where ancient fence lines intersect

The Mother Prairie sees the stones

forgotten on this primal atoll.

Where summers golden breakers on the wide wheat sea

and winters dormant fallow

year by year erode the fragile shore

ever shrinking this tiny piece of native ground.

Disheveled lilacs stand the sentinel

Aging chaperones

Relics of a time when someone cared

Barrow stones

strewn like knuckle bones,

in thigh high grass.

Only weathered runes remain

carved in markers a century old

of lives forgotten

questions left unanswered

dreams unfulfilled.

Castaways

trapped in the silent stones

on a sepulchral atoll

in the sea of grass.

Who were they?

They

for whom nothing remains

but a forgotten graveyard epitaph?

They

whose memories were discarded

like obsolete ideas

obscured in the verdigris of time

They

the mothers and sons

and fathers and daughters

who lived here

laughed here

loved and died here

Who were they?

They were us.

Who were good people

a century

or a cemetery ago.

Her Used to Be

I was up in North Dakota

not so long ago.

Went to visit family

but mostly went to see my Mom

who's been here on this earth

ninety years and nine as I write this.

We took a drive up home one afternoon

she and I

Went through our town

remembering

all those places

from our used to be.

The Alice Fairway Store

where we lived and worked

that was the place

that we called home

for all those years.

And the church and school.

They're every one

morphed and changed it seems.

I hadn't seen our store
since Momma sold it
ten years or so ago.
Almost wish I hadn't
'cause the folks that own it now
don't keep it up
the way they should.

A hundred years Saint Henry's was our church.
Then
I forget the year exactly
two thousand three or four I think.
Someone said the parish was too small.
Wasn't cost efficient
for a priest to minister so few.
So they closed
the doors of our church
and in their arrogance
struck a mortal blow
to the soul of our Dakota town

Alice School was where we kids
all went through the grades
but they consolidated
small town education

back in seventy five or so
and closed the doors.
So they turned it to a senior center
those forty years ago
And when the population of our town
was mostly moving to the cemetery
it got changed again.
When our old school
got bought out by an outfit selling fertilizer
and seed that's certified.

The graveyard there in my home town
nestled by the remnant the old NP
is about the only thing that grew.
'Cause as the population in the town got smaller
at the cemetery the opposite was true.

So we stopped in there and said hello
to friends and family members
that had passed
Grandpa, Gramma and my Dad
Aunt Mildred and a bunch of others.
Feels a little strange to realize
that most of my relations
are resting there anymore.

We took the car then
Mom and I
out to the home place
five miles as the crow flies
to the west.
Saw right away
the roof had fallen in
on the lean-to on the barn
where Momma and her sisters
did the milking
three-quarter century ago
The rafters finally giving way
rotting through
from shingles that had never been replaced.

Momma stayed inside the car
while I looked through
the barn and shop and house.
She was cold she said
and it was warm there in the car.

And as I walked into the empty house
the house that for those sixty years
had always been so warm

and now that was so empty

and so very cold

I knew

I knew what Momma felt

back there in the town

and now out here at the farm.

She didn't want to see the now

she wanted to remember

all those OTHER thens.

She'd rather

sit there in the car where it was warm

close her eyes

and from her vantage point

of ninety years and nine

look back upon

her used to be.

Post Script

I Remember

I remember

sacking potatoes by the ton into number 12 bags

I remember

spreading oily red sawdust

and sweeping the floors

late Saturday nights in the store

I remember

rubbing Vicks Vapo-Rub

under my nose

and breathing through my mouth

to keep from smelling the stink

of month old sour cream

while washing out the bottles

we used for testing.

I remember

our Daddy almost never

getting to sit down with the family for a meal

because someone would come in the store.

I remember

lying in bed

listening to the floor in the store

creaking till midnight or even later.

I remember

tiny Christmas Trees

tiny because they had to sit up front

in the window of the store

so people could see them when driving by.

I remember

belly flopping sleds

under the Northern Lights

on the icy street in front.

I remember

touching my tongue to my sled

when it was 35 below

and having to carry it in the house to thaw

so I wouldn't rip off the tip

(when my Grandpa heard about it he thought it was pretty funny. And it
probably goes without saying that it only happened just the one time)

I remember

Midnight Mass

when it was thirty five below

and blizzards

that moaned and howled

like a living thing.

I remember

raiding apples from the trees

at Lester Wellentine's farm.

and building huts

in the grove at the edge of town.

I remember

hunting birds with my slingshot.

I hardly ever killed anything

and when I did

I always felt a little sad.

I remember

spending literally days

cutting the grass with old push mowers

on the baseball field

so we'd have a place to play

I remember

walking the tracks

to the railroad cut

through the prairie roll

and in wintertime

building entire cities

in the great huge snowdrifts there

I remember

brother Darrel

learning to hunt and trap

nurturing a love of the outdoors that became a life long joy.

I remember Mary

born with it in the marrow of her bones I think

a sensitivity and love of music

that seemed to ooze

from her very pores

climbing on the bench and playing piano

before she could even reach the keys

Putting on shows and plays

and because it was an unspoken rule

that guys were supposed to act that way

I remember

pretending I was bored to tears

at what deep inside

I thought was really great.

And I remember Ann

the baby

a dozen years younger than me

the little barefoot, blue eyed, blonde

being the "kid sister"

I pretended to ignore

Sister Ann had a special something

she seemed not to suffer from that North Dakota malady

of terminal shyness

while the rest of us were worrying if someone liked us

Ann was making a million friends

and she's doing it yet today.

And I remember me

I was the nerdy kid

who at the age of twelve

nailed a granary door fifteen feet up a tree

so he'd have a place to read…

undisturbed

The kid who killed a rabbit once

because thats what boy kids do in North Dakota

and then who went behind the barn and cried

so no one else would see.

I remember

summertime

and Fourth of July at the farm

croquet on the lawn and kitten ball in the yard

and fireworks after supper

as the sun was going down.

I remember

Saint Henry's Church

and First Communions and May Crownings and Midnight masses

and Easter Lilies and Saint Henrys' Day picnics

and Hunters Suppers and weddings and baptisms and funerals

I remember

Saturday night dances and baseball games and snaring gophers and

shoveling snow

and the itch of Barley chaff on my skin.

I remember

loving school but pretending I didn't

'cause it wasn't cool

and I remember

Mom and Dad

instilling in me a love of learning that's never waned

I remember

so many things

that simply are

no longer

and I remember
North Dakota

and I remember
home

but especially
I remember
A Place Called Alice

Respectfully submitted

Dennis McMahon

* 9 7 8 0 6 9 2 9 4 8 5 8 3 *